Sinful Pride

A Man's Kryptonite

Billy Zeh

Unless otherwise noted, all Scripture quotations are from the New Living Translation (NLT), Copyright © 1996, 2004, 2015 by Tyndale House Foundation. Used by permission of Tyndale House Publishers, Inc., Carol Stream, Illinois 60188. All rights reserved.

Cover design and interior design by Inksnatcher.com.

Printed in the United States of America.
LC record available at https://lccn.loc.gov
Library of Congress Cataloging-in-Publication Data
Names: Zeh, Billy, author
Title: Sinful Pride: A Man's Kryptonite /Billy Zeh
Subjects: | BISAC: RELIGION/Christian Living/Men's Interests. RELIGION/Christian Living/Professional Growth. BIOGRAPHY & AUTOBIOGRAPHY/General.

Description: First edition. | Brunswick, Georgia: Broken Road Press, 2023. | Summary: "*Sinful Pride* explores the downfall of successful public figures undone by pride, highlighting the transformative power of humility and true measure of success." —Provided by publisher.

Identifiers: LCCN 2023950676 | ISBN 979-8-9892323-1-4 (softcover) | 979-8-9892323-0-7 (hardcover) | 979-8-9892323-2-1 (e-book)

For information about special discounts for bulk purchases, please contact the author at SinfulPrideMinistries@gmail.com.

*"God resists the proud
but gives grace to the humble." (James 4:6)*

This book is dedicated to my Lord and Savior, Jesus Christ. I can do nothing, Holy Spirit, apart from Your wisdom and discernment.

CONTENTS

INTRODUCTION

"I am the greatest." One needn't be a boxing fan to recognize this champion's trademark line. Muhammad Ali, previously known as Cassius Clay, Jr., grew up in Louisville, Kentucky, and was a boxing champion and a bragger. In February 1964, he proclaimed that he was the "greatest ever," just before his world title fight against Sonny Liston. Nicknamed the "Louisville Lip," Ali frequently declared how great he was, boasting and mocking his opponents.

Near the end of his life, the three-time world heavyweight champion and social activist could no longer fight the battle of life alone. His mind and body deteriorating, the Lip could only give life's challenges lip service. The man who once told a national audience he didn't need anybody later required help to stand up, get to the bathroom, shower, and eat, requiring full-time home healthcare. His life some sixty years earlier was quite different.

Ali was twelve, middle school age, when he began to box. In his teens, Ali had stood defiantly against the draft and the Selective Service system, saying the world of oppressed people, poor people, Black militants, hippies, and draft resisters were rooting for him, not for the system. This angered authority figures. As he made his way through the amateur ranks, winning a gold medal in the 1960 Olympic games in Rome, he became increasingly arrogant and self-aggrandizing, repeatedly proclaiming in the ring that he floated like a butterfly, stung like a bee; that the world champ should be pretty like him!

Ali shamelessly predicted the round in which he intended to knock out an opponent, and the boxing world sneered when he did so. To make it worse, he bragged about each new boxing victory. The Bible warns "Don't rejoice when your enemies fall; don't be happy when they stumble. For the LORD will be displeased with you" (Proverbs 24:17–18). Trouble was Ali was not a man of God.

PRIDE HAS CONSEQUENCES

What manifested in Ali and took hold in his youth, I have seen take hold of middle and high school athletes today. Regardless of the sport, it's something that shows up repeatedly at practice and, sadly, also during games. Football, baseball, soccer, wrestling— you name it, it always surfaces. It's not on the roster, but it might as well have a jersey and a player number. It has its place among the players. Sinful pride. "It" boasts, "Throw it to me, coach. I'll catch it." It brags, "I can make those free throws." It talks smack: "You're weak. You ain't nothin'." It prophesies, "I can hit, coach. I'll drive it over deep center!" Sometimes its chance comes right away. And just as quick come the results.

At a dual meet, one wrestler sizes up his opponent on the far side. Boasting within earshot of his singlet-clad teammates, in the spirit of Muhammad Ali, he prophesies that his thirteen-year-old adversary will be pinned in thirty seconds. Incredible as it may seem, that's exactly what happens! The pin occurs just as forecast; the decisive hold is called thirty seconds into the match. The gymnasium goes ballistic! The referee hoists the beaming winner's hand in the air, and *she* couldn't be prouder! Feeling stupid and embarrassed, the defeated and dejected grappler stomps off the mat, headgear in hand, his teammates spewing smack.

Time and again athletes brag about their athletic and sports specific skills. How they can catch a 22-yard pass on the fly, kick game-winning field goals, or beat the safety on a corner route—only to drop the ball on the first play-action pass from a coach's arm.

There's nothing wrong with having a vision, planning your future or deciding where you'd like to be five, ten, or even twenty years from now. There's nothing wrong with wanting the opportunity to prove oneself. And there's nothing wrong with being confident, but the difference between being self-assured and narcissistic doesn't seem to be clearly defined by behavior alone. There's something more.

This boasting is not limited to athletes. I'm not suggesting that anytime someone—a beauty contestant on stage, a factory worker during a meeting with management, or an account executive during a meeting with a client—makes a prediction about the caliber of their performance they are doomed or failure is a certainty. The term "break a leg" has a different meaning in baseball than Broadway. Context matters.

A spiritual tipping point seems to surface when people of all ages and walks of life—be they celebrities, politicians, entertainers, or even church members—express their opinion, complain, judge others, make a comparison, or express a desire in a way that's less than humble. The expressed thoughts of these friends, family members, educators, and government employees may reflect a general attitude about subjects the critics are passionate about. But they are judgmental of them, and they do so publicly.

Once their prideful words are heard or even read, it's almost as if a plague, weakness, or distraction arrives in short order, taking up residence in them, their lives, and their circumstances for a seemingly random future assignment of embarrassment, failure, and chaos.

"God opposes the proud but gives grace to the humble." (James 4:6)

REPROBATE

Another factor that seems to strengthen the foothold of sinful pride in people's lives is how often they succumb to it. Their rants are repeated in the form of text messages, emails, letters, spoken words, and especially social media posts. There's no better place than social media to poke at a sports prediction, make fun of an opponent, or complain about issues that personally matter. It's been my experience that God will eventually let them have their way. Surely the Israelites would agree. *So beware. He may just give you over to a reprobate mind* (Romans 1:28).

A reprobate mind refers to a mindset that is morally corrupt and strongly against godly principles. It is often found in individuals who actively disregard the truth and indulge in wicked deeds, thereby inviting God's wrath upon themselves (as per Romans 1:18). In the New Testament, the term "reprobate" comes from the Greek term *adokimos,* which essentially means "unapproved" or "rejected." It implies a state of being worthless and fake, either literally or morally.

Paul made reference to two teachers who resisted the truth, in the same manner as Jannes and Jambres opposed Moses, stating that they possessed corrupted minds and false faith (2 Timothy 3:8). In this context, their reprobation was linked to their refusal to accept the truth. This was a consequence of their moral corruption. Similarly, in Titus, Paul mentioned individuals whose actions were reprehensible, asserting that despite their claims of knowing God, their lifestyles contradicted this claim. They were deemed repugnant, disobedient, and ineffective for any good deeds (Titus 1:16). As such, a reprobate mind can be defined as one that is morally degenerate and of no value.

Individuals with reprobate minds may possess some understanding of God and might even be aware of His commandments. Nonetheless, they lead lives that are defiled and show minimal interest in pleasing God. Their existence is marked by corruption and self-centeredness. They find ways to rationalize and accept their sinful behaviors. Those with reprobate minds lack the Spirit's guidance and live solely for their own interests. In essence, reprobates are those who have been forsaken by God, left to the fate of their own sinful desires.

A genuine Christian, someone who has wholeheartedly embraced Jesus Christ through faith, will not possess a reprobate mindset. This is because the former self, tainted with a reprobate mind, has been transformed into a new being: "The old life is gone; a new life has begun!" (2 Corinthians 5:17). As Christians, we are essentially new individuals. Our actions and words reflect this change, and our lives revolve around our Lord and Savior, Jesus Christ, and our dedication to serving Him. Moreover, if we are truly committed to our faith, we are guided by the Holy Spirit to lead a life that honors God (John 14:26).

GOD SEES ALL

God is omniscient. God hears what we say even when we are not speaking (Psalm 139:4). He sees all that we "say" nonverbally—body language, text messages, emails, social media posts—good or bad. The Bible warns us about claiming anything we have is of our own making (1 Corinthians 4:7). God will hold us accountable for every idle word we express privately or publicly (Matthew 12:36).

God is a loving Father to all who seek Him. However, a loving father disciplines his children in a loving way because he loves them. When we sincerely confess our sins, God forgives. Our future in heaven with Him remains secure. But decisions have consequences—good or bad. He will discipline those He loves because there's a consequence for sin and He doesn't want us to do it again. But for those who knowingly and repeatedly sin, there will be a point when God will no longer listen to them. But only *He* determines who they are and when He stops listening.

COMMON THREADS

Considerable time was spent researching the lives of those examined in this book. Months were spent examining articles, reading biographies, and watching documentaries about them, their families, and their lives. In so doing, I discovered they had some common threads, even though they didn't know each other.

One common thread I found was that people of note frequently had a faith background in their early years. One or both parents believed in God and shared their beliefs with their children. Some attended church regularly on Sundays, others joined youth groups or participated in church-organized activities during the week. Reading or referencing the Bible was common.

Economic hardship was another commonality, even poverty. In spite of frugal circumstances, all of them became very passionate about a goal, subject, or activity in their life they found challenging, exhilarating, and exciting—one that drew much applause, financial reward, and heartache.

The most significant commonality was their prideful estimate of themselves. From the outside looking in, they were outwardly successful: money; cars; homes; and national, if not international, recognition. But on the inside, these notables were using a different set of scales to compare and measure themselves against others, weigh success, and validate their opinions and choices. Their flawed scales cheated them out of enjoying the fruit of the Spirit: "love, joy, peace, patience, kindness, goodness, faithfulness, gentleness, and self-control" (Galatians 5:22–23).

Pride is:

the quality or state of being proud: such as

a. reasonable self-esteem: confidence and satisfaction in oneself...

b. pleasure that comes from some relationship, association, achievement, or possession that is seen as a source of honor, respect, etc. ...

c. exaggerated self-esteem : conceit

—Merriam-Webster Collegiate Dictionary[1]

What Your Eyes Feast On

Jesus said, "The eye is like a lamp that provides light for your body. When your eye is healthy, your whole body is filled with light" (Matthew 6:22). The Bible's depiction of sinful pride includes the cravings of "the eyes." This extends beyond merely the things we physically observe to also include those we visualize or set our "mental" gaze upon. It further includes the

[1] https://unabridged.merriam-webster.com/collegiate/pride

"pride of life" or immoral longings to be the center of attention. Sinful pride also denotes the tendency or practice of boasting about our own achievements. As humorously expressed by one individual, maintaining humility becomes challenging when you consider yourself superior. Jesus called such boasting a sin (Mark 7:22). He who knew no sin was exposed to this when he was tempted by the devil (Matthew 4:1–11).

Ali called himself the king of the world, and said he represented the truth. There is only one King. Read Isaiah 2:10–22 and notice how high a man's pride can rise and how low he can be brought down and humbled in the day of the LORD. "Human pride will be brought down, and human arrogance will be humbled. Only the LORD will be exalted on that day of judgment" (v. 11).

I invite you to read about some public figures in the following pages, and follow their journey as if you've encountered long-lost friends, but they don't recognize you and you don't recognize them. As you walk with them through their stories, you'll sense something familiar about them. As pieces of their lives are revealed, try to identify examples of sinful pride in them. You've probably heard them before. Or at least a variation. Maybe you've said them yourself. Just like me.

1

Ex Rev

His head smashed the windshield, his chest hammering the steering column on impact. His brother tried calling 9–1–1, but his cell phone had no service out in the desert, so he appealed to a few passing motorists, who were inching by to call for help. Finally, help was on the way. First were the sirens. Then patrol cars, lights flashing as they twisted along the serpentine road. The first officer administered CPR, but many minutes had passed....

***

Samuel Burl was born in the harsh winter of Yakima, Washington, but quickly moved with the family to the hellishly hot summers of Peoria, Illinois. Richard and Marie were raising their four sons on a missionary's earnings, and suffering came with the territory of doing the Lord's work of itinerant Pentecostal ministry.

Samuel got hit by a truck when he was three years old. The accident damaged 40 percent of his brain. He didn't experience any seizures, but he was also diagnosed as having grand mal epilepsy. There was speculation that he could begin to experience seizures around the age of forty—a long way off at the time. The brain trauma changed Samuel's personality. He went from being a very quiet, unassuming child to being a loud, outrageous, always-in-trouble kind of kid. He was always clowning, always unpredictable. But though he was never in serious trouble, the family got to know the police on a first-name basis.

Samuel's parents pastored a few churches in different states, earning very little to pay for everything their boys—Samuel, Richard Jr, Bill, and Kevin—needed. To save on rent, they sometimes had to live above a sanctuary, where hours earlier a baby was baptized, or a wedding or funeral held. Richard and Marie lived and breathed preaching, and the boys, to some extent, followed, testifying and singing along. Samuel Burl was on a good path. An ancient one.

The family was at one point living in subsidized housing in an area riddled by crime, near Samuel Burl's grandparents. Money was habitually tight. There were times when Samuel and his brother wore nightshirts to school with their jeans. That's when they moved into an old Methodist church their dad bought—a welcome respite. The spacious, three-story structure had twenty rooms. The family lived on the third floor, in former Sunday school rooms. Their father gave sermons on the first floor and fed the homeless in the basement. But their mother, Marie, found having unpredictable street people inside her home unsettling, and she wanted them out. Richard heard what her heart said. He relocated the meals to an old picnic table outside, where they gathered for sandwiches. Samuel deeply admired his father for doing this.

CHILDHOOD DREAMS AND HURTS

While growing up, young Samuel enjoyed watching television and movies. In fact, when he was eleven, he thought he might one day become an actor. His hero was the fictional Dr. Richard Kimble in the television series *The Fugitive*. According to older brother Bill, Samuel didn't just relate to the character, he thought he *was* Richard Kimble: Their family, like the fugitive doctor, was always on the move, looking for sanctuary. Each week, the wrongly convicted Kimble was always pursuing the one-armed man he saw leaving the scene of his wife's murder. Samuel was also in pursuit, chasing not another ball but peace and harmony, things which, following the accident, had eluded him.

Samuel Burl was just eleven when his parents divorced. To his shock and dismay, the judge never asked him or his brothers where they wanted to live. The court decided each parent would have one or two of the children, ordering Samuel and younger brother Kevin to stay with their mother. Young Samuel loved his dad and was left devastated by the new arrangements. Meanwhile, his father and older brother Bill moved six miles away.

Young Samuel protested mightily. He was hurting and wanted others to know it, so he acted out. Sometimes he would get in the back of the church, and while standing behind everyone, pull down his pants. Sometimes he would commandeer the piano and play "Ragtime" instead of a traditional hymn. It was in this season he began listening to comedy albums. He really liked those by Richard Pryor and his unbridled routines.

Little by little Samuel Burl became rebellious, and his parents worried about him. Like the compassionate, fugitive Doctor Kimble, Samuel needed a home to rest in, eat in, and ultimately serve others from. But living inside a church with the public routinely coming and going through the front door challenged his sense of security. His world was somewhat dark, and he developed a fascination for horror and began crafting dummies, along with a penchant for wearing all-black clothing.

LOSING HIS FATHER

Samuel attended East Peoria Community High School, but when he skipped school too many days, he joined his brother Bill at Pinecrest Bible Training Center in Salisbury Center, a nondenominational, three-year, unaccredited school about fifty miles from Utica, New York. He hadn't been there long when his beloved dad died at the age of sixty-three. After the funeral service, Samuel said something very odd: that he wouldn't live to be forty.

Someone had to take over their dad's ministry, and Samuel and his brothers followed in their father's footsteps by becoming Pentecostal preachers. Samuel also played the piano, sang, and mingled with churchgoers. But once again, Samuel was on a path he didn't choose. His mother married again—to another preacher—and moved to Tulsa, Oklahoma, with the boys. Eventually, Samuel and brother Bill got an apartment together in a government housing project.

Samuel Burl preached from age seventeen to twenty-four, honing his craft on his own experiences and opinions and delivering them, literally, in a fire-and-brimstone, screaming-in-your-face fashion. He didn't earn much from evangelizing, never earning more than five thousand dollars a year. In his mind he had been faithful to God, a faithful servant who deserved better. So he questioned God, asking him, "Why are you keeping me so poor?"

FOLLOW YOUR DREAMS

It's almost as if God said, "Okay, I am going to let you have your way" and gave control of Samuel's life over to him. Samuel got married and they stayed together for a few years. Samuel and Bill's relationship was more like that of a father and son than brothers, so when Samuel told Bill he was getting divorced a few years later, Bill encouraged him to search his heart and pursue his dreams. Samuel didn't hesitate. He wanted to go into comedy. Bill didn't see it coming, but in hindsight, he wasn't surprised. Samuel never went back to preaching.

Samuel Burl moved to Houston, Texas, where he started doing comedy in small clubs. At the Comedy Workshop Comedy Club, he joined the Texas Outlaw Comics, a local comedy group, but he felt his career was growing too slowly. Five years later, he moved to Los Angeles, hoping to find comedy work and find fame, but instead he began working as a doorman. He kept working toward his dream though. Comedy, he said, was therapy for him. It helped him deal with life.

A Big Breakthrough

Samuel Burl finally had a breakthrough opportunity in 1985, getting a spot on Rodney Dangerfield's *Ninth Annual Young Comedians Special* on HBO. A comedy reviewer for the *New York Times* named him as one of the standout comedians, describing Samuel Burl as having a unique style that could be characterized as brutally misogynistic. He further added that Samuel Burl's act included a bizarre and wild howl that could be seen as an expression of the frustrations of married life.

Samuel Burl and LA were made for each other. Occasionally, an established comedian came backstage to praise the young comic's routine. One of them had also lived in the port city of Peoria, and they shared some mutual friends. He and Samuel Burl developed a great relationship and occasionally shared cocaine. It would be his downfall.

On an episode of *Late Night with David Letterman*, Samuel Burl introduced himself to television audiences for the first time. Letterman jokingly cautioned viewers to brace themselves, and it turned out to be sound advice. Samuel Burl skillfully utilized his previous role as a Bible-thumping preacher to deliver a satirical and irreverent performance, cleverly targeting the Bible, Christianity, and infamous evangelist scandals of that era. This bold and audacious style of comedy catapulted Samuel Burl to stardom. People who witnessed his act were not taken aback when they spotted his personalized license plate as he sped by. On his Corvette plate were the words "EX REV."

Samuel Burl was soon living more of a rock star's life than that of a comic. To help make the transition in his career, he signed with Front Line Management, a top management firm with a rock 'n roll track record. Artistically, Samuel Burl was like a child entering a new playground called show business. But once he learned how games were played and his repertoire grew, his comedy changed. He transitioned away from sight gags and amusing personalities to humor based on concepts and information—the basics of effective ministry. Both required getting and maintaining people's attention.

Successful artists get their best material from actual experiences, and Samuel Burl was no exception. His monologues centered around his first two marriages, then stretched to other relationships and more of his life experiences. And it was his viewpoint the audience heard when it came to political material. He sounded angry on stage because he was. He would pace across the stage, recounting his latest flame who had stolen his heart. The ovations he got walking offstage seemingly could be heard for miles.

To begin with, he looked like someone who might unnerve you on a foggy, rainy night in

London. He would not be called a typical comic, much less look like a rock star. He was short, cherubic, and weighed as much as 275 pounds. His standard onstage look consisted of baggy T-shirts, a wafting exhibitionist's coat, and a beret, looking more like a set designer than an award-winning architect of comedy.

HIS SINFUL PRIDE

Samuel Burl began living a carnal life. He took the badly flawed position that if he was going to be excluded from heaven because of sin, he might as well miss it in a big way. When he performed sober and clean, Samuel was a comic genius. But even when he wasn't, he was still hilarious. Yet, there were also times when alcohol was the only way he could make it through his shows. Samuel kept company with drug dealers, drunks, and scroungers. Every month, Bill was sending him five hundred dollars for living expenses, until he made a surprise visit and learned his brother had been sleeping on bar tables and using cocaine.

Samuel's sinful pride of position took off as soon as he became famous. Every commercial flight was first class. When he partied too hard and missed a commercial flight, he'd just charter a private plane. He also spent thousands and thousands on limousines. Out on the road, if he played a small town, he'd rent a fully stocked limo and keep it for twenty-four hours. That way, after the streets rolled up early, Samuel and his gang could still party in comfort. They wouldn't even cruise around. They'd just sit, parked, getting wasted in front of Samuel's hotel.

Samuel had been making all the rounds and promoting himself, and Hollywood had finally accepted him. But his offstage reputation—as arrogant, obnoxious, and offensive—preceded him. And managers and agents kept their collective distance, yet they watched Samuel at the Comedy Store and laughed until their sides split. Many years passed before anybody signed him.

People sometimes wondered if Samuel Burl was ever concerned about writing jokes others considered off-limits. Like Jesus. Like graphic sexual content. Wasn't he afraid of going to hell? As a former pastor with Samuel, Bill was among those who winced. He suggested to Samuel that he didn't need to use profanity to be funny. But the star fired back, saying that they weren't in church anymore. The retort took Bill by surprise. Samuel liked to have fun and have it with the people around him. He delivered as advertised—a high-roller who liked to show off.

The drought without a contract was due largely to Samuel's belief that he alone was in charge of his image. He arrogantly resisted any suggestion to improve his image, declaring only he had the right to change it. Deep down he continued to resent the Hollywood establishment. Samuel had a high regard for his peers, but not for agents who came and went like airport taxis. A war raged inside him. Like rice paper, the line between love and hate was very thin.

But he also had a soft side few people saw. One night he ordered twenty large pizzas to feed the broke stand-up comics at the Comedy Store. On another night, he filled up a truck with some of his own furniture, then drove it to West Hollywood, where a piano player and his pregnant wife lived. They owned no furniture and Samuel felt sorry for them. When Samuel heard a struggling artist was in need, he loaned money and, on occasion, paid their rent.

Samuel was afraid of having a stroke, perhaps always having his own prediction of being dead by forty in mind, but the fear didn't seem to curb his lifestyle. By December 1986, the *Louder Than Hell* tour had turned into one endless party. But Samuel's popularity had began to wane. He was playing to crowds of about a thousand rather than the five thousand of previous years. Following a November concert tour, he had grossed just $10,000 per night, compared to an average $50,000 in years earlier.

TURNING LIFE AROUND

After five years of madness, Bill finally forced his brother to come clean or at least try to. Bill found him a rehab center in Malibu, and Samuel agreed to go. For Samuel, the experience was like being back in church. At the age of twenty-eight, he was inspired to change course. He had taken stock of his life and something, at least in his mind, wasn't right.

In April 1992, Samuel married again, in Las Vegas. He and his new bride—a dancer—honeymooned in Hawaii before returning to Los Angeles, where he needed to rehearse for a sold-out show the following week in Nevada.

The week was like any other. But a strange thing happened the following Friday. Marie flew into New Orleans to attend her son's concert at Tulane University. Following the show, everyone went back to the Hyatt. On the elevator ride to their rooms, she looked at her sons and shared a dream from a few nights earlier. In the dream, her late husband said that young Samuel would not live much longer and she should tell him to organize his affairs. Then the dream ended.

A week later Samuel Burl and his wife met with Bill and others in Barstow, halfway to Laughlin. Leaving in separate cars, Bill witnessed his brother collide head on with a pickup passing another car on the wrong side of the road. At the scene of the crash, Samuel appeared fine, with only minor visible facial wounds. But he didn't seem to be able to hear anyone. He kept moving around, so they eased him out of the car, then laid him on the ground. With no emergency help at hand, as Samuel lay on Highway 95, it wasn't Hollywood he turned to. Samuel cried out to the Lord.

His best friend, Carl LaBove, who had been in the following van, holding his head in his hands. Initially, [Burl] appeared to have suffered no serious injuries, but within minutes he suddenly said to no one in particular, "I don't want to die. I don't want to die."

LaBove later said, "it was as if he was having a conversation, talking to someone else, some unseen person."

Then there was a pause as if [Burl] was listening to the other person speak. Then he asked "But why?" and after another pause LaBove heard him clearly say: "Okay, okay, okay.'

LaBove said, "The last 'okay' was so soft and at peace ... Whatever voice was talking to him gave him the right answer and he just relaxed with it. He said it so sweet, like he was talking to someone he loved."

[Burl] then lost consciousness. Efforts to resuscitate him failed. [Burl] died at the scene from internal injuries. An autopsy found that he had suffered numerous traumatic injuries, including a dislocated neck, a torn aorta, and torn blood vessels in his abdominal cavity, which caused his death within minutes of the collision.

—PeoplePill, "American Comedian"*

An ambulance transported Samuel Burl's widow to the hospital in Needles, where she received treatment for her injuries and was then released. Friends and family were in denial, struggling to accept *how* he died. He was starting to settle down, going through detox, and living a normal life. In their minds, he wasn't doing anything wrong. So why did he die? One old friend tried to make sense of it all, reasoning that Samuel was simply on his way to work when he died. They were puzzled that he died while living by their definition a clean life, and not from a drug overdose or some guilt-ridden pleasure.

Confirmed by the coroner's office, the comedian hadn't overdosed, but trace amounts of cocaine *were* found in his system. This news surprised his friends and family, especially Bill, given his brother had allegedly stopped using drugs after his irregular heartbeat was discovered. But there was more. Small amounts of codeine, Valium, and Xanax were also found in his system. The other driver—a seventeen-year-old—survived the accident. His blood test revealed toxic levels of alcohol in his system.

On Samuel Burl's tombstone is written: "In another time and place he would have been called prophet." One nationally known radio talk show host, known himself to push decency to the edge, said of Samuel: "To write him off as some bizarre, untalented party animal overlooks the obvious. He was a genius."

Samuel Burl was rightly nominated in 1988 for a Grammy Award and a posthumous award for Best Spoken Comedy Album in 1994.

The comedian performed without fear. In the world of comedy, he was a combination of aviation pioneer Jimmy Doolittle and tightrope walker Nik Wallenda. Most people go to the edge and then stop. Not these guys. And certainly not Samuel. He, like Doolittle, pushed his craft to the edge and plunged into the valley of unknown results. And like Wallenda, Samuel kept his eye on the other end, where success awaited. He didn't allow the risk to dictate the outcome. The scream Samuel Burl Kinison was noted for was never set off in the face of impending disaster. Rather, it was part of the act. It proclaimed that Grammy award-winning, stand-up comic Sam Kinison was on his journey home.

RESOURCES

Amy Wallace, "Friends Shocked by Violent Death of Mellower Kinison: Entertainer: The shock comedian was sobering up, associates say. A teen-ager is held in the collision." *Los Angeles Times*, April 12, 1992.

Bill Kinison, *Brother Sam: The Short Spectacular Life of Sam Kinison*. New York: William Morrow and Company, 1994.

David Handelman, "The Devil and Sam Kinison: The preacher turned heavy metal comedian spreads his unholy gospel, but can he conquer his own demons?" *Rolling Stone*, February 23, 1989.

Dennis McLellan, "Kinison's Friends Recall His More Compassionate Acts." *Los Angeles Times*, September 2, 1992; updated June 26, 2023.

Julie Seabaugh, "Sam Kinison's Wild Ride, in Part 2 of her massive oral history of the larger-than-life comedian, Julie Seabaugh chronicles the highs and lows of his popular years, his attempts to get clean, and his death 15 years ago this month, on the road to Laughlin." *Las Vegas Weekly*, April 12, 2007.

Leo Benedictus, "Comedy gold: Sam Kinison's Breaking the Rules: He came from a family of Pentecostal preachers and performed comedy with righteous, thrilling fervour." *The Guardian*, December 20, 2012.

*"Sam Kinison." *Peoplepill.com*, n.d., Accessed November 6, 2023.

How to Know God

Dear Sinner: You were created to know God personally—to maintain a relationship with Him, through His Son, Jesus Christ. How do you begin a relationship with God?

1. <u>Admit</u> that you are a sinner. "For everyone has sinned; we all fall short of God's glorious standard (Romans 3:23)." You are not defined by your past.

   No matter how good we think we are, we all fall incredibly short of being a good person. This is because we are all sinners. The Bible says "only God is truly good" (Luke 18:19).

   We cannot become who we are supposed to be without Jesus Christ.

2. <u>Believe</u> that Jesus Christ died on the cross for you. "But God showed his great love for us by sending Christ to die for us while we were still sinners" (Romans 5:8). This is the good news, that God loves us so much that He gave His only Son to die in our place when we least deserved it (John 3:16).

   The Bible states, "Repent of your sins and turn to God, so that your sins may be wiped away. Then times of refreshment will come from the presence of the Lord " (Acts 3:19–20). The word "repent" means to change our direction in life.

Instead of running from God, we can run toward Him.

3. <u>Confess</u> Jesus Christ into your life. "For everyone who calls on the name of the LORD will be saved" (Romans 10:13).

   Becoming a Christian is more than going to church. It is having an ongoing, personal relationship with Jesus Christ, in your life and heart. Jesus said, "Look! I stand at the door and knock. If you hear my voice and open the door, I will come in" (Revelation 3:20).

To have a personal relationship with Jesus Christ, first get down on your knees. If you are not physically able to do so, humble your heart before the Lord. Then, sincerely pray out loud, the prayer below and mean it in your heart:

> Dear Lord Jesus,
> I know I am a sinner.
> I believe You died for my sins.
> Right now, I turn from my sins.
> and open the door of my heart and life.
> I confess You as my personal Lord and Savior.
> Thank You for saving me. Amen.

Did you pray this prayer?

If you said yes, you are now born again! Your old life is dead. You have been made new. You are a new creation in Christ Jesus. Congratulations! You have received the free gift of eternal life.

We want to send you a copy of the Beginner's Bible free of charge! For more information and to receive your copy, email your name and address to SinfulPrideMinistries@gmail.com.

2

───∞───

SHOCKA

In and around Jackson, Michigan, along the I–94 corridor, people are blessed to say they know him. Kevins' town, Jackson, with its tree lined neighborhoods, is a small town where people look out for each other. The town—called by some the birthplace of the Republican Party—is populated with farmhouses, row homes, and historic Sears Roebuck catalog homes. The Grand River, Michigan's longest river flows right through the city limits. And in that town is also the park, where one young man learned how to play football. Kevin's story and the spotlight it put on Jackson gives many of the area's residents a reason to be proud.

***

Kevin was born on a cool October day in Jackson, the former auto industry town thirty-five miles south of Lansing. The future coach was one of four children, and parents Wilbur and Cleomae prioritized faith and education while raising them. During World War II, Wilbur had been one of the famous Tuskegee Airmen, but in Kevin's childhood, Dad was a science professor and his mother taught high school English.

Playing in Bloomfield Park, a small park on Jackson's Michigan Avenue, "Shocka," as his young friends called him, was once a sore loser. But that changed as he developed an attitude of gratitude. Kevin learned not only to be a good teammate but a good friend as well. He pursued everything with excellence, both his studies and his football, and his natural leadership qualities caused friends to always want to play on his side in a game.

At Frost Junior High, several of the same friends were on his middle school football team, and they still looked up to the future NFL Hall of Fame member. Many would call and go over their football homework with him at night, gaining clarity on what they were supposed to do on each play. Later they'd played high school football together.

An honors student and outstanding athlete, at fourteen, Kevin was elected Parkside High School's student body president, where he also excelled in basketball, football, and track. Kevin started his sophomore season at Parkside High as quarterback in the season opener. There could be five guys huddled together and Kevin would not have played a single down with any of them. But he had the ability to bring a group of guys together and make a team.

Kevin's high school football coach was so impressed by Kevin's advanced understanding of the game that he gave him the team's playbook. Kevin not only studied and memorized the playbook, he also diagrammed the plays and then taught them to the team. Football was Kevin's passion. Even outside of high school, he and his friends would get a bunch of guys together, pool their gas money, and head to Lansing to play ball. He loved football that much.

PROFESSIONAL

After graduating from high school, Kevin became the quarterback for the University of Minnesota's Golden Gophers. During his sophomore year, he led the team in the first three games, but his performance was hampered by injuries. In the third match of the 1974 season, he suffered a ligament strain in his left knee, and a shoulder injury further limited his effectiveness. Despite enduring these injuries throughout the season, he managed to rack up 417 yards on the ground and 612 yards through the air, totaling 1,029 yards. His resilience and performance earned him the title of the team's Most Valuable Quarterback for two consecutive years.

Kevin was more than an athlete. He received the Big Ten Medal of Honor—an accolade that acknowledges one student athlete from the graduating class of each Big Ten-member institution—in recognition of his outstanding performance in sports coupled with academic excellence throughout his collegiate journey.

His success came as no surprise to the folks back home. They had seen Kevin doing what he could to positively impact not only his family but also his neighborhood. His job, in his mind, was to help people better themselves.

Kevin was overlooked in the NFL draft, but that didn't deter him from playing professional football. He became a free agent with the Pittsburgh Steelers, playing defensive back for three seasons. In his best year he recorded six interceptions, and earned a championship ring in Super Bowl XIII.

Kevin holds the unique distinction of being among the few players to have both intercepted a pass and thrown an interception in the same match. In a game against the Houston Oilers, Kevin was thrust into the quarterback position when both the starting and second-string quarterback left the game with injuries.

COACH

Kevin was twenty-eight when he was hired as defensive backfield coach for the Steelers, and thirty when he was promoted to defensive coordinator.

During this time, Kevin was set up on a blind date by his pastor. Unwilling to court him at first because of Kevin being an athlete, Laura and her parents were completely surprised when he showed up for her dinner date. He didn't look at all like the football player they had imagined, much less sound like one. Turned out he was more like Steve Urkel. Softspoken. Wore prescription glasses, and was generally mild-mannered. They got married a year later.

Following a losing season, team owner Dan Rooney strongly encouraged the head coach to make staff changes, and Kevin was demoted back to his original position. Kevin considered the downgrade a test of faith. He believed God gives tests to see if his children would stand firm in the faith and keep believing when things didn't go the way they'd hoped.

He began studying the coaching style of Joe Gibbs, then head coach of the Washington Redskins, whose teams won three Super Bowls in eleven years. What intrigued Kevin was the Redskins thrived in the midst of the most challenging of environments, especially the playoffs, when the pressure was at its highest. Kevin observed Gibbs and spoke with people who knew him, learning that Gibbs's objectives were to win football games, but winning was never Gibb's only purpose; he also wanted people to see biblical principles in action—in himself as well as the Redskins.

HEAD COACH

One January, Tampa Bay owner Rich McKay was looking to take his chronically unsuccessful team in a new direction. He hired Kevin as head coach to reorganize the Buccaneers. A successful career in the National Football League was a dream come true and came with money, notoriety, and accolades. Kevin would live that dream, and he coached the Tampa Bay Buccaneers from a losing position to a regular spot in the playoffs.

Everything looked like it was going well. Armed with a new defensive coordinator, Kevin implemented a form of the Cover 2 defense with a few twists. Kevin used a smothering zone defense, which employed a base formation of four linemen, three linebackers, and four defensive backs.

The linemen were ready to rush the passer while the cornerbacks would cover the passing flat area. The linebackers protected the middle of the field, and the safeties protected their own zones. The defensive plan was not a new one, but Kevin expanded the defense into a system used in every down situation. He was very intentional in choosing players and methods to execute the defense, resulting in his defensive style that earned the title the "Tampa 2" around the league.

Whatever Kevin started he would finish. On the field he wasn't necessarily the best athlete, but it could be strongly argued he was the most analytical. Kevin's innovative approach to coaching helped extend one free agent's career. The disillusioned veteran was interested in resigning. Kevin's hiring changed that. He saw a man of integrity and character in Kevin and stayed.

Kevin learned that it takes every one of the team's fifty-three players to win and that every player on the roster should get the same level of training. This became the foundation of Kevin's coaching philosophy. He believed teams should always have a well-thought-out strategy to account for any possible injury or substitution in the game and the strength to keep going, no matter what.

Success started showing up at the games. Kevin led them to the playoffs four times in six seasons. The Buccaneers first appearance in the championship Super Bowl game occurred six years after Kevin became their head coach, and the Buccaneers won Super Bowl XXXVII.

FIRED

But missing from the celebration was Kevin, fired after the prior season for never getting the team to the championship. Ironically, he was credited for building the heart of the team that won the Lombardi Trophy, and he'd left a firm foundation for his successor.

Kevin coached the way he wanted others to coach him. Other coaches who have studied his philosophy have followed suit and learned different approaches to winning, in ways that challenge conventional wisdom. Kevin acknowledged that his approach to coaching cost him more than a few job opportunities, when he was looking for his next job. Headhunters were looking for the stereotypical coach who demanded perfection from players, who would show emotion and everything the culture expected in a head coach. But that wasn't him.

It's not uncommon for football players to thank God when they score a field goal, kick an extra point, or score a touchdown. But what is less common is obvious praise when things go wrong. A pass is dropped, the ball fumbled in the end zone, or a game-winning kick misses the uprights. Kevin believed fans watch players' reactions with more interest when there's a setback versus when there's a victory. Kevin taught the players he mentored to express gratitude no matter what the instant replay reveals, nor the score at the end of the game.

People could not see who Kevin was beyond their perceptions of his personality or how he was going to coach well. For a coach's faith and family to be more important to him than a job and seven-figure salary were difficult concepts. He was the exception—a rare coach who refused to put down players, publicly or otherwise. He made his point each time a player needed to hear it and then moved on. He had the players' respect, and they knew not to challenge him. His players felt if they didn't accomplish what they set out to do, his feelings would be hurt, which was something they didn't want to do.

MOVING ON

When the league expanded to thirty-two teams, it also realigned divisions. The NFL's American Football Conference (AFC) South Division had the same members from the beginning, and following another cold, dark, so-so season, the Indianapolis Colts were looking to heat things up in the league.

Starting from the top down, Kevin was appointed head coach, tasked with transforming a team known for its sizzling offense and, unfortunately, its sparkler-like fizzling defense that lit up but didn't last long. He'd inherited a scoring machine that operated at a very high level, so no noticeable changes were made there, and it was in the hands of the retained offensive coordinator—someone he knew and trusted. In sport it's been said that the best offense is a good defense.

Transitioning from balmy Tampa Bay, Kevin got right to work rebuilding the defense, adopting the "Tampa 2" scheme and fine-tuning it a little more each season. But Kevin struggled to rehabilitate the Colts' defense, and the post-season results gave little hope. In a first-round playoff game, the Colts lost to the New York Jets, and the team went on to lose post-season contests.

And then the unthinkable: Kevin's eighteen-year-old son committed suicide, plunging Kevin and his wife into the darkest days of their lives.

There would be no set time for recovery. There never is. He didn't know if he would ever be okay. Christmas would never be the same. No steroid shot could mask this kind of pain. But over time, Kevin found he could still function. The desire to change came on its own. There was no epiphany. It was simply time to move on.

But after taking a leave of absence, Kevin didn't quit, knowing the young men on the team needed him. After all, they were like his family too. The Colts didn't give up on him either, signing Kevin to a three-year contract extension. They believed in his coaching methods and trusted him to do what was best for the team. The strength that Kevin demonstrated following his son's suicide was an inspiration for others dealing with similar loss.

COACHING STYLE

One player described Kevin's coaching style as the way Jesus would coach. It was Jesus's relationship with the disciples that taught Kevin how to lead. In turn, the disciples learned to love one another. The more time they spent with him, the more the players saw the heart of a champion. They saw the way someone who followed Jesus should coach a team. Kevin was an easygoing leader whom detractors misunderstood because he rarely yelled and screamed at players. His critics wrongly interpreted his self-control and self-discipline as a sign of weakness. On the contrary, he was very disciplined conversationally and exercised the importance of detail. This quiet strength never gave place to panic.

Kevin believed that coaches are basically teachers. Teaching his players was something he enjoyed as a coach. He would pray for opportunities to impact someone's life. He wanted to go beyond "What's up" and keep walking. He wanted to find out what was going on in their lives. He intentionally got to know the players and understand what their needs were. He believed that instead of yelling, screaming, and jerking a player's helmet by the grill, he should care for the player first. He dismantled any preconceived behavioral concept of how a coach is supposed to act.

PRIDE

But in spite of his strong marriage, his deep faith, and his quiet coaching, Kevin's pride in what he believed a referee should have called nearly destroyed his playing career during one game. It happened when he complained there was a conspiracy—one he couldn't prove—and he angrily let the referee know in a threatening way. All his sinful pride did was get him ejected from the game. As he sat alone in the locker room, the game played on. What had his anger accomplished? He vowed to God and himself to never let his emotions rule him again.

Kevin's pride could have kept him stuck in a mindset of anger and judgment, thinking himself better than others. That didn't happen. He acknowledged his anger and determined to let God lead him forward in humility.

The following season, the Colts' playoff run was characterized by greatly improved defensive play. They won against the Kansas City Chiefs and then the Baltimore Ravens in the next round.

SEVEN-YEAR RUN

Kevin had an incredible seven-year run with the Colts, and thanks to his leadership, the team became a regular Super Bowl contender. The following season in 2007 they won the AFC title and made it to the Super Bowl XLI, creating history with their huge comeback.

The Vince Lombardi Trophy finally came Kevin's way in Super Bowl XLI—the organization's first in more than thirty years and the first since moving from Baltimore. The winning team hoisted the trophy in the air to terrific excitement. But when the thrill was over and the newness had worn away, Kevin questioned its value in the Ella Sharpe Museum or in a closet full of awards. He knew that what he and his family needed wouldn't fit on their mantle. Those trophies he'd lain down much earlier. Ultimately, the outcome of an old, rugged cross was at their core, not a trophy, and he lay down any pride that might have built inside him from winning.

RETIREMENT

Kevin coached two more seasons before humbly retiring his coaching clipboard. But Kevin still had his doubters, despite his Super Bowl wins, and he started searching for deeper meaning to his life. Could God use him to help others as he had when he walked along Jackson's brick-lined sidewalks?

Kevin's lowest days were after his oldest son's— Jamie's—suicide. Particularly interesting to Kevin was learning that young people who are actively involved in athletics are less likely to commit suicide than non-athletes. Already active in many community service organizations, such as the Fellowship of Christian Athletes (FCA) and Athletes in Action, Kevin knew he could help athletes through mentoring.

Kevin and wife Lauren, an early childhood education specialist and former teacher, love the kids they mentor, and to this day believe they can guide them through life. Furthermore, their declared faith in Jesus Christ is the foundation and driving force in their life for all their activities in and outside of football.

In August 2007, Kevin was nominated by President George W. Bush to be a member of the President's Council on Service and Civic Participation. The position was one for which Kevin felt unworthy. When he went into coaching football, the last thing he expected was to get a presidential appointment for anything.

Interestingly, in a 2019 unpublished paper "Religion and College Football: The Success of the Christian Coach," researcher and football coach John Bennett of Valdosta State University concluded that "[C]ollege football coaches who have publicly proclaimed to be Christians have won 13/14 of the past thirty National Championships titles. It is no wonder that godly humility leads to heavenly success.

BEST SELLERS

One weekend Kevin's parents and his uncle came to Florida for a two-day fishing trip. They had fished freshwater only once before. A charter boat waited, worried Tarpon to pursue, in brilliant sun rarely seen in Jackson. Two days just relaxing and not worrying about the ones, like championships, which got away. While on the water, Kevin decided to write a book.

When he mentioned it to a few friends, they encouraged him to do it, which turned out to be good advice. Kevin's memoir, *Quiet Strength* became a *New York Times* best seller twice, and it was the first NFL-related book that sold so well. The Lord's timing was perfect.

A great source of fulfillment for Kevin isn't from winning the National Football League championship but from the success of his books. He quickly learned that his encouragement and wisdom could spread further and faster on paper than through mentoring. He was deeply moved by letters from people helped by his writings and whose lives were changed, especially many young men in prison. Kevin's books gave them hope. The fact is people learn a lot more from trials, tribulation, and defeats than when everything is going along just hunky-dory, and the death of his son had caused him to let God carry him in his anguish. Kevin writes that there's no better time to pray than when you're at your lowest point—to humble yourself before God and ask Him what He is trying to show you, what you can learn from this, and how He can help.

TODAY

Anthony Kevin Dungy, known to American football fans as Tony Dungy, fills his days in part with a variety of nonprofit groups, focusing on families and faith, as well as with his television work during the NFL season. He knows personally that true happiness comes from humble service, not having all the answers, and certainly not from living in pride.

Now married more than forty-years, Anthony Kevin and Lauren have raised a large family of three biological children and eight more adopted. They have fostered 100 children.

"Sacrifice and offering You did not desire; My ears You have opened. Burnt offering and sin offering You did not require."
(Hebrews 10:6 NKJV)

RESOURCES

Adelle M. Banks, "Tony and Lauren Dungy: On faith and family, football and race, winning and losing." *Churchleaders.com*, August 8, 2022.

Art Stricklin, "Tony Dungy voices the pain & lessons from his son's suicide." *Baptist Press,* February 4, 2006, Baptist Press.com.

Biography.com Editors, *Tony Dungy Biography. Biography.com*, n.d., Updated March 29, 2021.

Chip Mundy, "Former NFL Coach Tony Dungy thanks hometown of Jackson during Michigan Sports Hall of Fame induction speech." *Jackson Sports*, Feb. 19, 2013.

Jerry Green, "Pride Of Jackson, Mich., Now Coach Of Buccaneers." *Detroit News*, November 30, 1997.

John Romano, "In a world of turmoil, Tony Dungy still trusts the human heart." *Tampa Bay Times,* June 19, 2020; Updated June 20, 2020.

Peter King, "A Father's Wish: There Was One More Person with Whom Tony Dungy Wanted to Share His Landmark Victory." *Sports Illustrated,* February 12, 2007.

Tony Dungy, *Uncommon*, Tyndale House Publishers, 2023.

WHEN GOD ALLOWS SUFFERING

Tony Dungy did not have all the answers. But there were things that he did know: God's promises are in the Bible. God is in control. God promises that good will result from suffering.

The valley being traveled in may be incredibly difficult and painful. But those going through tragedy can find comfort in knowing that God has a plan of restoration. Survivors or victims of tragedy may not get to see any results this side of heaven. Nevertheless, God is working through and in you. Your life matters! Jesus will walk beside you. Likewise, God is not abandoning you in the midst of your darkest hour. You might not see a miracle on the level of Lazarus, but God understands your pain, is with you, and desires to comfort you in your suffering. God promises eternity for His children.

We serve a God of mystery. There's a mystery that seems to come with suffering, with faith (1 Timothy 3:16), with creation. But God's answers to questions and the problems of life can be found in the Bible and through Jesus Christ.

Compassion can be found in suffering. Jesus said, "I was hungry, and you fed me. I was thirsty, and you gave me a drink. I was a stranger, and you invited me into your home. I was naked, and you gave me clothing. I was sick, and you cared for me. I was in prison, and you visited me" (Matthew 25:35–36). When a hurricane, tornado, or flood sweeps through a community, many helpers and nonprofits come forward. Compassion is seen in action.

The message of unity through hardship is often present. Frequently, children are brought back together and witness restoration amid their trials.

Suffering carries a message of comfort. It is written,

> All praise to God, the Father of our Lord Jesus Christ. God is our merciful Father and the source of all comfort. He comforts us in all our troubles so that we can comfort others. When they are troubled, we will be able to give them the same comfort God has given us. (2 Corinthians 1: 3–4)

Because you have experienced suffering, you have more understanding for those who also suffer and can feel more empathy for what they're going through. The Word of God has comforted you and you can pass on the comfort He gave you.

It is completely natural to ask why God would allow something like suicide to happen, why there is so much pain in this world, and why you have been affected while others seem to have it easy.

WHAT IF?

Within a short space of time after being created by God, man turned around and acted as if they had no need of Him anymore. God warned them that they couldn't survive without Him, which has proven itself to be true. Whatever the cause of man's death, his spirit lives on, so your destiny depends on your relationship with God.

Any problems in life we face and go through are because there is sin in the world, and when we rebel against God, the act opens our bodies to affliction. Yet God has made a way for us to be free of sin forever through Christ's death on the cross. He died with our sin and rose free of its shackles.

Suppose God had spoken with Kevin before Jamie's death and said Jamie's death would help many people, would lead to their redemption, and would pay the penalty for their sins. But there was one condition: He would have to take Jamie. No father could agree with that. Yet God did, giving His own Son for our sake 2,000 years earlier, giving every man the choice to have eternal life. That's the benefit Kevin, Lauren, Jamie, and the rest of their family share. Anyone receive the free gift of eternal life if they ask Jesus to come into their heart and be their Lord and Savior.

Kevin's biggest regret is not hugging his son goodbye—his last goodbye—when James left after being at home for Thanksgiving. Kevin never wants to have the same regret again, so everywhere he speaks, he leads his audience in a prayer of salvation, inviting those who do not follow Jesus to accept Him as their Lord and Savior.

If you have not yet done so, accept Him as your Lord and Savior today.

3

---∞---

SODDY

A passenger can see a lot of the world from the vantage point of a railroad car. But David's worldview is, one might say, a *little* different. When he's not on the world's stage, he prefers HO scale—model railroading, that is. Twice he has been on the cover of *Model Railroader,* a position more meaningful than any cover of *Rolling Stone.* When the first article came out about the layout he'd built on the top floor of his Los Angeles home, the response was extraordinary. People everywhere were surprised and delighted that someone of his notoriety is unashamedly a rail or model railroad enthusiast, and not only that, he has a diploma designating him as a Master Model Railroader from the National Model Railroad Association of America.

Oddly enough, it is not trains themselves that interest him. David's not a train watcher, nor is he an authority on types of locomotives. What fascinates David is the detailing of the miniature city. Its grimy buildings. Potholed streets. He creates, with few exceptions, all the pieces. Getting the landscaping around the railroad tracks right so they look real. The world disappears when he is working on it.

David's interest in model railroading can be traced to when he was seven and got his first train set consisting of Tri-ang track and an electric train. Even when the electronics burned out, he still pushed the train around the track. Later, in his teens, he built a layout on a board 6' x 4'. But he got sidetracked when his dad bought him his first guitar. He didn't pick up the hobby again until his father retired and his parents moved to a different house a few blocks away.

Like passenger trains, David's world is almost always orchestrated, but sometimes hectic and not always on schedule. There was even a season when artificial substances were his ticket to ride between performances. Nowadays, David leaves the artificial world of entertainment and returns to his hotel room as quickly as possible. There he conducts a strange harmony of a blaring train whistle, the clickity-clack of a passing freight train, the clanging of a rail crossing's warning bells, and the crossing arms swinging into place. He enjoys the same solitude savored by hobbyists everywhere. When so much of his life is orchestrated by others, he likes the idea of being able to control a few things. He's not only the director but the conductor as well, inspecting the model train cars and dictating what's going on in and around them. His life is finally full.

***

David's story began as the war in Europe was painfully drawing to a conclusion, albeit a grim one. London was, in a sense, lifeless, far from being resurrected back to pre-war life. Large areas had been devastated by the Luftwaffe, food was rationed, and winters were bitterly cold. Nevertheless, warm celebrations would erupt occasionally, adding much needed light to a dark outlook. That was the case one January, when Robert and Elsie were blessed with a new baby boy, David.

In the middle of World War II, Robert, a Scottish man, and Elsie, a North Londoner, were shocked to discover Elsie was pregnant again, as they'd thought their family was complete after having their four children in Scotland and then moving to Highgate, but they were happy about it all the same. Where they lived was another story: They were living on the edge of town and stayed there out of financial necessity, but their home was adjacent to a target favored by the bombers—the railroad yards— making their house more susceptible to a misguided bomb. From the outside, the boarded-up windows made their home look vacant. The windows had been blown out so many times from the concussion of exploding German bombs that David's dad had given up replacing them. Various bombs—the V1 Buzzbomb, then the V2 rockets—fell all around the family during Elsie's pregnancy.

Thousands of Londoners were faced with a dilemma: stay in harm's way in the city or split the family up and evacuate the children to rural areas largely out of harm's way, where they would be temporarily adopted by other families. Being separated from one another simply was not an option for David's family. If one were to go, they would all go, so not one of them did.

It wasn't uncommon for the air raid sirens to wail at 1:30 in the morning, forcing the couple and their sixteen-year-old, Mary, ten-year-old Bob, and nine-year-old Peggy out of bed. Coats on and pillows in hand, Elsie and Robert led them in the dark to the Anderson bomb shelter in the garden—six sheets of government-issued corrugated iron formed into a shed and sunk halfway into the ground. Dirt and sandbags blanketed the roof for added bomb proofing. Then all three children wriggled their way into narrow metal bunkbeds and tried to sleep until morning. Only fifteen-year-old Don remained in the house . . . unless the walls began to shake. Then that fourth bomb shelter bunkbed became simply irresistible.

Life improved once the war ended. By some standards, they were poor, but David always felt well fed and happy. The youngest child tends to get spoiled and David was no exception.

SCHOOL

In primary school, David showed little interest in music. Even in secondary school, it's surprising to think the one thing that petrified David more than anything else was standing up and singing in Mr. Wainwright's music class. To be clear, it wasn't because he was shy. It was the idea of being singled out and mocked that he despised. His answer: The Fake Sick Trick.

To pull off the trick, he needed one empty meat sauce can, a small amount of mashed potato, a small number of carrots, and water scraped from the side of his school lunch plate. Using any available utensil, he mixed it all together. When the chance came, he stealthily took the gunk outside to the playground and tossed it unnoticed to the blacktop. The stage was now set. Pointing to the splattered ground, David called to the teacher on duty nearby. "I'm sick," he reported. Mission accomplished, and excused from music, David headed home. Or was it to the movies?

EARLY DAYS

One by one, all David's older siblings left home after Ron. Mary got married first, then Peggy, then Bob. They may have moved out, but they didn't move far, occupying houses and apartments just doors away. Just like in war times, they stuck together. David's loyalty to his family was legendary.

It seemed that David was frequently in the right place at the right time, even at the young age of eleven. During a men's soccer game one Saturday morning, David was hanging around near the fields, as usual, where the Highgate Redwing sides were playing. When the reserve team realized they were a player short, the adults huddled together, then turned in unison toward the kid standing on the sideline. Someone handed David a spare black-and-white-striped jersey, which he quickly put on. It hung on him so long, it looked like a dress. What happened next should be in soccer history. Fourteen minutes into the first half, David scored a tap-in from two feet away. His teammates erupted in celebration at their young teammate's goal. It was a game-changing moment in David's life, one he replayed over and over again in his field of dreams.

It was in secondary school when others saw David had some shine to his soccer game. He gained playing experience on junior teams before becoming captain of the Middlesex Schoolboys, playing center-half. He was a good, all-around athlete who even tried his hand at cricket, but soccer remained his real love. On the Middlesex roster with David were the Davies brothers, Ray and Dave, and Pete Quaife, who not only enjoyed playing soccer but also enjoyed playing music. The trio would later take their place on the world's stage known as The Kinks.

MUSICAL BEGINNINGS AND WORK ETHIC

Elsie was more outgoing than Robert. She was a very good mother, and she loved family gatherings and everyone getting up and singing a song. David was very reluctant to sing, but little by little and encouraged by his brothers and sisters, David's interest in music grew.

It wasn't until he turned thirteen that he bought his first record, Eddie Cochran's *C'Mon Everybody*. A year later, his dad presented him with a surprise gift, a used electric guitar. In short order, David started to believe in his musical talent and joined his first teenage group, who he played with outside of school hours.

Like many his age, David had no idea what his future looked like. When Robert turned sixty-five, and David was in his early teens, he retired from the building trade and bought and opened a newsagent's shop. The family lived in the apartment above it. When he wasn't playing with the Kool Kats, David worked in the newsstand. He also delivered papers in the early morning, but found getting up on time proved a challenge to prompt newspaper deliveries. Elsie woke him frequently, only to find him still asleep an hour later. On another occasion he got up, threw the newspapers over the railway, and went back to bed.

But David developed a deep love and respect for his dad while working with him in a job that lasted for half a decade. David valued loyalty and honesty, traits he inherited from his thoughtful father—a quiet man who was somewhat puritanical. David's biggest worry was upsetting him, and nothing was nearer and dearer to David's heart than their relationship.

David's greatest asset was his unbeatable belief in himself. When the first group he joined didn't work out at the age of fifteen, he joined another called the Kool Kats. He also quit school in the hope of becoming a professional soccer player, but that didn't pan out, so he fell back on his music.

But in spite of his pride in his musical skills, David learned, as many others before him, that the music business can be cruel, if not disappointing. He learned this brutal lesson with a group called The Raiders. He was invited to sing some extra tracks with the band while it recorded an instrumental song called "Night of the Vampire," but as he was singing around the band, trying to get accustomed to them and vice versa, the producer overseeing the project brought David's first recording opportunity to an early finish in a dramatic way ... he charged into the studio and booed in David's direction. But David wasn't about to give up that easily.

Next, David learned how to play the harmonica and tried the nowhere man life of a traveling musician. Borrowing some money, he and his pals set out to see the world, walking three miles to Waterloo station, where they caught the train to Brighton and did a few shows. Then they took the ferry to France. The boys hitchhiked to Paris and David hit the town running at six every morning to busk. He wasn't alone with his dreams. Other entertainers had followed a similar route, heading to Paris only to find the entertainment strip saturated. So, David changed direction and headed to Spain, only to find even fewer opportunities. When his money ran out, he found sleeping quarters under Barcelona's football stadium. Before long, the Spanish police arrived, and David was thrown out of the country for vagrancy, along with a few more strapped-for-cash traveling minstrels. At the police station, the British Consulate was asked to help repatriate David back to his family in Highgate and give him a bath—the first in weeks for the prodigal son.

OH SUSANNAH—LOSING A CHILD THROUGH PRIDE

David was just seventeen when he met Susannah—a well-spoken, middle class art student. A year later, he was in disbelief. She said she was pregnant. He thought she was joking, but the expression on her face said otherwise. They had been having fun, taking weekend trips to the beach, cuddling up in railway passenger cars, then walking arm-in-arm along the boardwalk. On Saturday nights, they would sometimes sleep under a bridge overpass near the beach. That's when the baby was conceived.

Disbelief immediately left the field and fear of the baby's impact replaced it, beginning to dominate the game of their lives. David knew getting a girl pregnant out of wedlock would bring shame to his family, and he was terrified of Robert and Elsie's reaction to the news. Nothing he had ever done before would compare to this. But David's pride rose up to where he decided he couldn't humble himself before his parents. "Why cause *them* shame?" he projected. He was also stone broke, with no way to provide for a child. So, he chose to keep the pregnancy from his parents.

Again, David let his pride about wanting a job title override any decision about raising his own daughter. Fortunately, Susannah chose life. She carried their baby girl, Sarah, to term and placed her for adoption. Bob was the only family member David told. Susannah and David split up soon after. For the rest of his life, he would carry lots of guilt.

It's no surprise that such a shock to the system would make a man change a lot about himself. For David, his hairstyle was the first thing to change dramatically, and he started to spike his hair. This would become his trademark look.

LONDON NIGHTLIFE AND A BREAK

David frequented London's nightclub scene for the next few years, even getting to play harmonica with one group once a week in Studio 51 and doing the odd bit of vocals with the Dimensions. He also enjoyed The Crawdaddy Club, which was nothing more than the back room of an English bar. It was a popular, crowded venue, where people danced and had a blast listening to groups like The Yardbirds, who rocked them to get over-under-sideways-down to the incredible guitar music of future superstar Eric Clapton.

David's big break came in 1964, after leaving an R'n'B performance by Long John Baldry's Hoochie Coochie Men at the Eel Pie Island Club on the Thames River at Twickenham. Following the show, David made his way to Twickenham station to catch the train home, making himself at home on a bench before he blew a few sad notes from his harmonica into the cold evening air. Waiting on the opposite side of the platform was another man trying to get home. He, too, had hurried away from the Eel Pie. Standing in the cold, he heard down the platform a harmonica riff from "Smokestack Lightning." The sound was coming from an obscure character wearing a black leather jacket and bundled up in scarves like a mummy. Moments later the 6', 7" blues singer Baldry introduced himself, explaining he was always looking for new talent, and asked David if he'd like to join a jam session the following Wednesday.

David jumped at the opportunity, but as a minor, Baldry needed Robert and Elsie's permission. Baldry got the impression they were dead set against David pursuing a singing career. But after a while, they saw how happy David was, more so than doing any nine-to-five job he'd ever had. David negotiated a contract with Baldry that would pay him ten percent of everything the band earned. Based on how many gigs they played, which varied from night to night, David's wages worked out to about $30 a week. It wasn't exactly a fortune, but David felt it was a decent amount for singing a song, then introducing Baldry. There were two shows, so he would sing twice. The problem was David had no signature song. The second problem: there was no time to rehearse. It is an understatement to say David's first session didn't go well.

SPEEDING TO FAILURE

Though David had sung before, he had no experience singing solo. Baldry told him not to worry, just to stand in front of the mic and sing. Well intended, but it did little to alleviate David's nervousness and the feeling of being sick to his stomach. Seeing how on edge he was, another band member told him not to worry and handed him a black-and-white pill called Black Bomber. David, who knew little about drugs, gulped down the "speed." For a few minutes he felt no change. But by the time he took the stage, his eyes had become like plates. He soon felt six feet off the ground.

The band began the intro to Ray Charles' version of "Nighttime Is the Right Time," a rhythm and blues song held together by signals between singer and musicians. As the song progresses, the momentum builds. It has no clear end point, so it can potentially go on forever. But this train had no conductor. David was high as a kite. Instead of bringing the song to an end, he yelled to the band to continue another six minutes before they pulled the emergency cord. The audience was torn between applause and throwing rotten tomatoes. Besides being awake for a full three days after, David felt dejected and tempted to give up. His pride in his abilities caused him to think that he couldn't show his face again because he would have to be humble about it, and God forbid that he should fail at singing! But he let a little humility leak in and determined to get better.

HUMILITY WINS

Baldry eventually found he could duet with David, and the youngster's place in the Hoochie Coochie Men was secured. So was his repertoire of solo songs, which grew to include Muddy Waters' "Tiger In Your Tank." Still, he didn't consider himself a blues singer. He was a folk singer at heart.

As their reputation grew, so did their following. The Hoochie Coochie Men found themselves booked every night of the week, sometimes with three gigs a night on weekends. They were especially popular in the counties in northern England, so the band traveled a lot. The band's travel was hardly glamorous, with David taking his turn in the back of Baldry's old yellow warehouse truck.

The band became a second family to David. They played well together, at times very well, but traveling was harder—they toured in the cramped seating of a van for hours on end, days at a time, with performances in between set the table for sniping at each other. David drew the resentment of the others by always being the first to head to the bathroom when they parked. He did this not because of an urgent need to relieve himself, but to check his trademark hair. It was something he had in common with Her Majesty, the Queen—both maintained the same hairstyle for forty-five years and longer.

GOING SOLO

Musically, Baldry was good for David. The two built a strong friendship that remained solid in the sixties, and David's debut recording was on the B side of Baldry's "Up Above My Head." John Rowlands and Geoff Wright saw his potential as a solo act and offered to manage him. David was very interested in the offer, but he wisely did not immediately sign a contract. He had taken to heart warnings that the recording industry was full of sharks, and he wasn't about to swim alone. Of greater importance to David was maintaining his friendship with Baldry and his financial arrangement with the band.

When the budding singer approached him about the management offer, Baldry could not have been more cordial and encouraging. Himself under management, Baldry gave the go-ahead and David signed with the duo, but not before adding a clause that prevented his new managers from staking a claim in any work he had done with Baldry and the band. He parted ways with the Hoochie Coochie Men two weeks later, which was a good move as they were about to break up and Baldry was filing for bankruptcy.

David's new managers went right to work trying to get a record deal. Armed with a demo, Rowlands and Wright visited several record labels, only to be turned away. David's voice was "too rough" or "gravel sounding" and had little chance of success, most labels said. Except for one. Mike Vernon of Decca Records—who also signed the Rolling Stones) heard the demo. After some negotiations, he agreed to produce a single.

Even by rock star standards, David was still pretty awful. Musically, he was still a novice. He could barely get his voice to carry a twelve-bar blues. But he had no fear. Now called "Rod the Mod," he played with Steampacket for a while, then jumped into the cover band Shotgun Express with organist Beryl Marsden, guitarist Peter Green, and a drummer named Mick Fleetwood—collectively the forerunner of the group Fleetwood Mac. A year later, he joined the Jeff Beck Group, who he toured with in the USA and Europe, followed by some years with Faces, where his career took off.

FACES

Faces' onstage and offstage antics of wild parties, alcohol, groupies, trashed hotel rooms, and vandalism were legendary, resulting in their being blacklisted by many hotels. None of these practices were very smart from a financial perspective. The band was continually having to pay large amounts of money to cover the cost of damaged hotels and discourage managers from calling the police. Yet, in all the debauchery, David found time to write music. He had been in the business for seven years, and insiders were beginning to doubt if he would ever make it.

In the early 1970s, the Beatles had largely come and gone, but the Rolling Stones were still trying to find satisfaction around the globe. Every band David had been a part of no longer existed, but he remained undeterred. David compiled, sang, and produced an entire long-play record for Mercury Records. His was a distinctive sound. His voice had its own character that resonated with audiences. He didn't just know how to sing a song; he knew how to *dwell* in the song and make it his. It was his coming-of-age when he demonstrated his prowess as a singer and songwriter.

David once said slamming his fingers in a door was preferable to writing lyrics and putting them to music. It didn't come easy. For example, he would have a song title but no idea what the song was about. The process began with humming a few sounds, uttering a few noises or notes, then adding words to fill in the gaps. He eventually came up with lyrics, but he could not explain where they came from. It was as if he found a lamp for his feet, a light for his path. His lyrics often originated from his past experiences, like opening a diary and singing from it, which forced him to relive the shame he felt being forced to sing in front of Mr. Wainwright. The shame lasted for years. He was so self-conscious of his feelings about new lyrics from an old sin that he would clear out everyone from the studio except the engineer.

The shame didn't stop him from dating, though, and he got very close to Swedish film actress Britt Ekland. She had a profound impact on him, and they had pet names for each other: he called her Poopy and she called him Soddy. It was her idea for David to wear makeup during performances—possibly a nod to the reviews David Bowie was getting at the time. David credited her with broadening his perspective about art and a number of other subjects, but that all ended when she discovered he was seeing someone else.

David continued his pinball dating journey, rolling from one relationship to another as often as he did clubs.

LOSING IT ALL

Over time Faces' reputation spread to other countries, including England. Their earnings grew too, but they eventually broke up in 1976, after which David went solo and continued to build his fame and fortune, his song "Do Ya Think I'm Sexy" a firm favorite around the world. He also got married to Alana Hamilton in 1979. He still sang with Faces. The problem was that Faces had no bookkeeping or money management. And it all went belly up in 1982. David's pride had elevated him to supreme heights only to have someone he trusted implicitly take it all away.

It all got to be too much. By 1984, David was divorced with two children from the marriage.

A Voice Scare

David was very fit. He worked out daily, performed shows, and still played soccer on the weekends. But then a routine physical revealed the need to surgically remove a nodule near his thyroid, and even six months post-surgery, he couldn't sing. He could only muster a sandpaper-like sound. To David, they were some of the longest weeks of his life, and he had to wonder if it was time to bring this chapter to a close.

He recalled something Grammy winner Sting said. If his career ended tomorrow—if the music died, the money was gone, and the fame disappeared like dust in the wind—he'd be happy living again as he did at the beginning—in a one room flat. Where your treasure is, there your heart will be. David didn't know if he could rise to that challenge. What other work would be as satisfying?

Then David made a tactical decision that would change the course of everything. For weeks he had been waiting for his voice to return on its own without change. What if he was to force the issue? If he messed up his vocal cords and things got worse, what difference would it make? What was the worst that could happen? His strategy was twofold. He recalled the surgeon explaining how it had been necessary to cut through the throat muscles in order to remove the cancer. With time they would mend but lose their muscle memory. In short, they would forget how to sing. They would need to be retrained.

Someone told him of a cantor at a nearby synagogue who knew everything about voice training, and he was able to start therapy sessions immediately to strengthen the throat muscles. Soon David could sing a complete song uninterrupted. The second part of the plan involved the band. The idea was for David to try to sing until his voice gave out each day. Weeks later they were doing an entire show. David's appreciation for the band grew with each practice. They, like other close friends, had shown extraordinary patience with him, later saying that their shared belief in God caused them to form a strong spiritual bond that helped David through.

But it took a Lamb to get the real healing started. His voice was new. It still had its trademark raspy sound, just new and improved. But something was still missing. David was drinking with friends at the

Dorchester Hotel and taking stock of his life. On the rebound from divorcing his second wife, he made a vow to himself that he wouldn't rush into yet another short dating experience or marriage. The next one would be for life.

MORE SCARES

After a concert one evening, David got on a plane, ready to relax. Suddenly, right after takeoff, there was a loud bang from the port side. The plane hit a bird, knocking out one of two engines. As the plane lost altitude, David's thoughts turned to dying. He had just sung before thirty thousand screaming fans. Now he was the one screaming. Where would he spend eternity? He didn't know.

The pilot was able to turn around and by God's grace, the plane landed without incident. But it wasn't until the next day when David realized the hand of God was in the event. Only the day before the emergency, the pilot had taken a refresher course on how to control a plane in the event of engine loss!

LIFETIME LOVE?

Penny Lancaster was a tall, blonde model and professional photographer who David found drop-dead gorgeous. But there was something different about this encounter. For the first time he felt attracted to a woman beyond her outward appearance. *This* shiny Penny was warm and genuine.

Despite his bass player trying to derail their connection for months, they eventually had their Kodak moment, but over the ensuing months, David saw Penny just a few times. That's because she was engaged. David realized Penny needed time alone to choose between them, but he wasn't going to be the one who forced it. Torn between two lovers, she walked down to the lake nearby. Sitting beside the still waters, a large, white waterbird drifting nearby suddenly took flight. A moment later, a single white feather floated down and came to rest next to her. She saw this as the answer she was looking for—she would choose David.

She was almost thirty-three when David asked her to marry him, dropping on one knee in the Eiffel Tower. The following June, they were married, white feathers in the décor as a reminder that God had used a waterbird's feather to show Penny the way to this point in her life. They have two sons together. David finds it a challenge to fully recall the tremendous joy he has had from his children. For David, it is all a blessing. No record sales compare to that, nor will they ever.

Their marriage remains strong, despite a prostate cancer scare in 2017. Every now and then Penny will take a look at the white feather that fell beside her that day at the lake. Holding it reminds her of the pure love they have for each other, united in one flesh. For David and Penny, 9/11 changed a lot about their lives. They started attending church more frequently. They prayed to be more authentic. While on tour even now, if they see a church with its doors open, they will sometimes stop in and pray. They give thanks to God for everything and express their gratitude for each other.

Groups of people still clamor to see David around the world, but he takes no pride in that. His favorite group is found right at home. His family, especially on Father's Day, means more to him than Christmas or even his birthday. Some of his children, now adults themselves, live thousands of miles away, while Alastair and Aiden are home every day. David looks forward to hearing all his children's words of love. They are all he wants to hear.

"What will it profit a man if he gains the whole world, and loses his own soul?"
(Mark 8:36 NKJV)

Nowadays, David can be all he wants to be. He doesn't have to put on a show, even though he still does. He doesn't have to worry about selling records or meeting with record company executives. He can be Roderick David Stewart, better known to model railroaders and lovers of pop music everywhere as Rod Stewart.

RESOURCES

Alan Burke, "Rod Stewart takes in city's 'Downtown Train.'" *The Salem News*, December 7, 2013.

Nicole Lampert, Daily Mail Showbusiness Editor, "Now Rod's found God," *Evening Standard*, July 14, 2005.

Rod Stewart, *Rod: The Autobiography*. New York: Crown Archetype, 2012.

Tim Ewbank, *Rod Stewart: a biography*. London: Headliner, 1994.

WILL GOD MEET YOUR NEEDS?

God knows we have needs: food, clothing, and shelter, and He promises to those in Christ that He will supply them from His riches. However, sometimes we have needs created by ourselves. In the parable of the prodigal son (Luke 15:13–18), the youngest son asked for his inheritance and chose to leave his father's house, eventually ending up in the pig pens and broke. How did he get there? By choosing to leave the very best and making some very bad decisions. Wrong needs are created by disobedience, rebellion, blame, accusation, and sinful desires which lead to wrong decisions. Decisions have consequences: good or bad.

Sometimes we have needs created by the needs of others. Charles Stanley told the story of a twenty-four-year-old woman who said she was an adult child whose mother was mentally ill and hospitalized most of her life. Her father was an alcoholic who sexually and physically abused her. She hated God because of her circumstances. What is the source of her needs? She didn't do this herself. Her emotions were deeply marred and damaged by someone else. She felt worthless, shameful, guilty, and incompetent. Emotions set like anchor points in her mind.

Many like her have kept these hurts to themselves and tried to bury them and move on. But all this does is let the hurt build up inside, till it becomes part of the memory. No matter where she went or what she was doing, she had a hatred of God. Kids who grow up in broken homes have needs created by others.

Sometimes we have needs created by God. Consider a family that has a new home, great job, nice neighborhood, schools, etc. They have gotten settled into their routines when the husband suddenly announces he's feeling called to preach. "What does this mean," his wife asks. The husband says he'll need go to seminary. "What does that mean?" she continues. We're going to have to sell the house, move to a seminary, and build a new life.

The family's list of needs looks something like this: The father needs to explain how he's been called by God. He needs to explain to the children why they have to move and leave the comfort of their friends and school. The couple need to sell the house and get another one while he's in seminary. The father, perhaps the mother as well, needs to look for a job to provide for the family. It is important to understand the father didn't choose this on his own; God called him, God created the need, and God will provide for every need He created in their lives.

Stanley also said we have needs God created to accomplish His purpose and plan for our lives. "Lord! You could have stopped _____." Sometimes God allows or creates things to happen that He could have stopped. He's sovereign. He has charge over everything. But He allows heartache, disappointment, hardship, hurt, criticism, persecution, and rejection for His purposes.

4

ICONOCLAST

Gasping and wheezing, Stephen's sweaty hand clutched at the couch as he lowered himself to lie down. From beyond the room, he could still hear the sound of scattered applause. His heart was pounding, and he could feel the gears grinding in his chest. The pressure was beginning to rise again. He closed his eyes and waited.

***

Childhood sweethearts Jim and Lorna lived in Bethesda, Maryland, when Stephen was born, the youngest of their eleven children. And what a house of kindness it was. Jim was an immunologist at the National Institute of Health in D.C., and Lorna, who once dreamed of being an actress, was now a star homemaker.

When Stephen was still a child, the family moved from their suburban home in Washington, D.C. to the suburbs of Charleston, South Carolina, where

Jim worked at the medical university. For Lorna, corralling the kids was like being a captain in charge of the crew on a Murrell's Inlet trawler. Keeping track of her deckhands while they were out to sea required that Lorna and Jim view their family from a wheelhouse using the power of prayer and GPS (God's Positioning System).

It took some doing, but Lorna managed to keep track of them all, whether they were up at bat, on their toes in ballet, or wading in the pluff mud of a tidal creek. The rambunctious Stephen and his siblings were much like any other kids growing up on the water; walking and riding bikes on the island's dirt roads to go fishing, crabbing, shrimping or to just hang out under a live oak or sweating Spanish moss in the humid South.

Away from the water, Stephen was a big fan of Alfred E. Newman, and he was regularly wading through *MAD* magazine and its outrageously funny satire. He liked performing for his siblings and they enjoyed his MAD-inspired one-act plays. Stephen also loved school, though that was mostly because he had a massive crush on Ms. Katsos, his fourth grade teacher. Homework and classwork though? Not so much. Sadly, when he was ten, she moved away, and though the loss of his favorite teacher was a hard blow to take, it did little to prepare him for what would come next.

That Saturday was probably like most any other on James Island. Partly cloudy. Mid-70s. An Atlantic ocean breeze wafting through at fifteen knots. But no one in Stephen's family saw the storm coming that would rip their family apart. Spring storms can form quickly along the Atlantic coast. Skies become overcast and wind pick up. Stephen's father and his two teenage brothers, Peter and Paul, were flying enroute from Charleston to Charlotte when the plane lost altitude and was swallowed by the fog, crashing in a North Carolina cornfield. Stephen later told *GQ* article writer Aurelie Corinthios, "Nothing made any sense after my father and my brothers died. I kind of just shut off."

Rocked by this tragedy, Lorna moved the family to downtown Charleston. Every window of their new home had a view of the harbor, giving Lorna and the kids a new outlook. But the move opened a secondary wound for ten-year-old Stephen. Gone were the guys he'd grown up with. Making matters worse, he was an outsider to the rest of the neighborhood, and the kids there never accepted him. With his remaining siblings working or away at school, Stephen became his mother's constant companion. He saw her walk by faith and not by sight. Stephen still has her crucifix hanging on his wall.

Stephen was a '70s music kid, but his musical tastes were also shaped by his older siblings, who savored songs from the '50s, '60s and '70s. While other fourth graders were watching *Fat Albert and the Cosby Kids,* Stephen listened to his siblings' lively discussions about Vietnam, Watergate, and Kent State because they had been away at college protesting about them.

Life for the others seemed to go on, but not for Stephen. He just wasn't the same. To fill the emptiness, he turned to "Dungeons & Dragons" spending hours on the fantasy game with anyone who would play. He also began to read, and soon fell in love with science fiction.

High school was an unhappy time for Stephen as well. He felt like an island. Detached. Alone. He quit playing sports and joined the drama club, where he really enjoyed acting, but a question still plagued him; Why, Lord? His parents had been devout Catholics all their lives, and Stephen was an altar boy but still harbored doubts about his faith. He didn't understand why God would allow these things to happen. Lorna told the children they could question, even challenge, church practices and still be Catholic, so he felt free to question God's ways.

COLLEGE

In 1982, Stephen was accepted to Hampden–Sydney College in Virginia to study philosophy. He also continued to participate in plays, but he found the core courses challenging. Nevertheless, he decided it was time to get serious, so he knuckled down academically, became more disciplined, and worked harder.

The theater community at Hampden–Sydney didn't draw a lot of attention, but that didn't hinder Stephen's growing interest in acting. Two years later he transferred to Northwestern, majoring in theater and studying performance. One cold, wintry Chicago day, he was out for a walk when someone handed him a New Testament Bible with Psalms and Proverbs. The little book was quite stiff, and he had to force it against his leg to open it. The Bible broke open to a verse that Stephen would credit with restoring his faith in God: "Do not worry about tomorrow, for tomorrow will take care of itself. Each day has enough troubles of its own" (Matthew 6:34 NCB). The words of Jesus seemed to speak from the page. He felt the burden he'd been carrying for so long leave him immediately. Then, an epiphany. Giving thanks to God energized the young comic to accept with love the world God had given him, even the sad parts.

The apostle Paul said that we can be sure that every detail in our lives is worked by God into something good (Romans 8:28). In our suffering in the weeks, months, even years that follow, we may not feel that way. Stephen later said that one of the heartbreaking aspects of someone huge in your life disappearing in a moment is not knowing what happened, but his new connection with God helped him in his long-term grief.

As Yogi Berra said, "When you come to a fork in the road, take it." Now in his mid-twenties, Stephen found himself at a fork of his own. His girlfriend had issued him an ultimatum: sink or swim, fish or cut bait. He needed time to think, so back to Charleston he went, seeking his mother's wise counsel. If there is any doubt, she told Stephen, don't do it. Something happened then that made Stephen's decision for him.

A DIVINE APPOINTMENT

The annual Spoleto Festival in Charleston was underway, so that evening Stephen and his mother went to see one of the shows. When they walked into the lobby, he immediately noticed a woman standing across the room and thought, *That one, right there.* Then he thought, *This is crazy. You're crazy!* Crazy as it sounded, he knew instantly that he had just seen the woman he would one day marry.

After the show he saw her again in a food line. He was going to get his food and walk away, but something told him that if he didn't introduce himself to the mystery woman, he would regret it. So he humbled himself, rustled up some courage, and went over and said hello. Her name was Evelyn

McGee, and he spent the rest of the evening talking with her, amazed to discover they had grown up just two blocks apart. Moreover, their families knew each other. Three years later they married.

PANIC

Things were moving along nicely for Stephen and Evelyn, while he took various acting roles, until Stephen's closest friends and stage partners, who had been working with him at Second City—the improv and comedy training theater in Chicago—moved away to New York. Their move was devasting for Stephen. Their departure from his life could be likened to a theoretical breakup of Abbott leaving Costello, Lucy without Ricky. For years they had talked and collaborated daily; now he was completely alone and spiraling.

Without their support, a lie from the enemy crept in, robbing him of his confidence. Believing he had thrown his life away by gambling on his career choice caused his anxiety to rise. So pervasive were the panic attacks that he briefly took prescription medication, feeling uncertain he would ever create again. He had allowed his source of joy and fulfillment to become too dependent upon his identity as a successful comedian. His confidence unraveling, he would go onstage, perform, then curl up in a ball backstage. Then he would uncurl, go onstage again, and feel fine. Offstage, he would fall apart once more. This vicious cycle went on for months, but no one seemed to notice.

Freshwater fishermen sometimes use a throwline to catch fish, and Stephen desperately needed to grab hold of one now. It took some time, but eventually Stephen realized his affliction served a purpose. Like the apostle Paul's thorn in the flesh, God allowed Stephen's panic attacks to play a role as change agents along a dark, broken road period in his life. They were, in a way, motivators to create new material. One morning he awoke to discover the feelings of panic were gone, and he knew he had the answer; he had to perform.

CAREER

Stephen's public persona loves performing, even singing occasionally; but away from all the lights, camera, action, it's obvious Stephen has another side. It's the face of a "regular guy" who lives a normal life, feasting on Low County Boil, going to church with his family most Sundays, or helping his son with a Boy Scout project. Stephen maintains a healthy divide between his personal and professional lives. He gives 100 percent onstage but afterwards refocuses on what really matters: his family. He loves being just another dad in the suburbs.

Stephen considers himself very blessed to be able to do what few people do, and to keep at for so long. He's received numerous awards not only his work, but also for his efforts to improve the lives of others through nonprofit organizations. His net worth is reportedly $110 million dollars, and he's extremely popular within the entertainment industry. However, Stephen's level of success, if left unchecked can lead to a false sense of immunity, as if the words one says have no real consequences.

Stephen has described himself as an iconoclast of sorts. When "in character," he boasts of tearing down public figures, attacking religion, and exploiting current events. His political satire, sarcasm, and comedic treatment of local, state, and federal officials is critically acclaimed. Few of those targeted by his assaults get to sit opposite him onstage and share their own worldviews, so the scales of justice become tipped and uneven. One must wonder if Stephen, an occasional Sunday school teacher, ever considers the consequences of violating the Bible verse: "Let no corrupting talk come out of your mouths, but only such as is good for building up, as fits the occasion, that it may give grace to those who hear" (Ephesians 4:29 ESV).

Stephen and Evelyn filtered what their kids watched on television. Significantly, they didn't allow the children to watch their dad at work, reasoning they couldn't understand irony nor sarcasm and didn't want them to perceive their dad as insincere. But Stephen wasn't concerned with his viewers' perceptions and their responses to each day's jokes. How they reacted was their reality, he said. The only reaction he cared about were those that affected his ratings. For example, mocking Donald Trump had been good for Stephen's ratings.

ELECTION NIGHT

Prior to election night, Stephen, his writers, producers, and others had enthusiastically forecast a landslide victory for Hillary Clinton, whom Stephen and other pundits promoted and showered with praise and adoration. Trump, on the other hand, was constantly lampooned by Stephen and virtually every major media outlet, declaring practically in unison that the political novice, billionaire international businessman, and star of the massively successful television program *The Apprentice* had zero chance of winning the election. A team may be winning the game at halftime, but it's never a good idea to laugh at your opponent before the final score. More than one team has overcome a deficit to win the game. He who laughs last, laughs best. "Spouting off before listening to the facts is both shameful and foolish" (Proverbs 18:13).

Stephen later said that the election night live show was the hardest thing he'd ever done in his life. His team had lined up several guests and prerecorded many segments for the show based on Hillary winning and had never considered that Trump might win. Enough material for close to three shows was scrapped forever.

From the moment Donald Trump announced his candidacy, Stephen and the production company had written one-liners, sarcastic monologues, and skits mocking and ridiculing him. They invited like-minded guests to the show who shared their contempt for the man, even expressing their hope for the candidate's demise. For nearly two years, the ridicule was nonstop. In his sinful pride, Stephen and his associates had heavily invested in what they hoped for—their opponent's downfall—and the outcome of the election would be key to their late-night ratings success. The downfall they hoped and planned for went well beyond an election. Just like a man in the Bible named Haman.

HAMAN

Haman is first mentioned in Esther 3:5–6 as a foe of Mordecai and the Jewish people:

When Haman saw that Mordecai would not bow down or show him respect, he was filled with rage. He had learned of Mordecai's nationality, so he decided it was not enough to lay hands on Mordecai alone. Instead, he looked for a way to destroy all the Jews throughout the entire empire of Xerxes.

Haman, a trusted advisor of King Xerxes (also known as Ahasuerus), used his royal influence to enact a law ordering the annihilation of the Jews. To make Mordecai a spectacle, Haman erected a gallows approximately 75 feet tall to hang him on (Esther 5:14).

However, divine intervention reversed the situation. King Xerxes, unaware of Haman's hatred of Mordecai, ordered Mordecai to be recognized for preventing an assassination attempt on the king. To Haman's dismay, he was ordered to lead Mordecai through the city on horseback, declaring the king's commendation (Esther 6:10–11).

Queen Esther, who was Jewish herself, invited both the king and Haman to two feasts. Unaware of the queen's heritage, Haman considered this a great honor. Haman's plot was revealed, "so they hanged Haman on the gallows that he had prepared for Mordecai. Then the wrath of the king abated" (Esther 7:9–10 ESV). Haman's animosity towards the Jews led to his own demise, proving the truth of Proverbs 26:27.

"If you set a trap for others, you will get caught in it yourself. If you roll a boulder on others, it will crush you instead."

On the designated day of the Jews' destruction, it was their adversaries who met their end (Esther 9:6–10, 16). Haman's ten sons were also executed (v. 14). Haman's life serves as a warning of the fate that awaits those who oppose God and His people. It didn't work for Haman, Antiochus Epiphanes, or Adolph Hitler, and it won't work for the Antichrist.

SOMEONE ELSE'S GALLOWS

Back in today's Hollywood and the fantasy world of entertainment, Stephen Tyrone Colbert, the host of *The Late Show,* metaphorically experienced a similar death. He had proudly orchestrated a multiyear harangue against a man exercising his constitutional right to run for public office. A right that Stephen Colbert himself enjoyed. Colbert had planned extensively to celebrate what he predicted would be the inevitable political death of the man he had crucified onstage week after week.

The Late Show with Stephen Colbert was the most-watched late-night show in total viewers for the 2020-21 television season—its fifth consecutive year at the top. Now it is in sixth place (September 2023).

Colbert let his pride and celebrity hang him from the very gallows he had enthusiastically constructed for someone else, and he is the one who ended up looking like a fool.

Those who wish to boast
should boast in this alone:
that they truly know me and understand that
I am the Lord
who demonstrates unfailing love
and who brings justice and righteousness to the
earth,
and that I delight in these things.
(Jeremiah 9:24)

RESOURCES

Aurelie Corinthios, "Stephen Colbert on Learning to Accept the Deaths of His Father and Brothers: 'I Love the Thing That I Most Wish Had Not Happened.'" *GQ Magazine*, August 18, 2015.

Bryce Donovan, "Great Charlestonian? ... Or the greatest Charlestonian? Stephen Colbert." *The Post and Courier,* January 8, 2007:

web.archive.org/web/2007010813225 /www.colbertsheroes.org/articles/CharlestonPost -Apr29-06.shtml.

James Martin, "Faith in Focus: Stephen Colbert on faith, God and politics in the age of Trump." Faith in Focus, 2019.

www.youtube.com/watch?v=DDDCQIaEsHE&t= 846s.

Jordan Zakarin, "Stephen Colbert: The Tragic Plane Crash That Changed His Life." *Biography.com*, October 28, 2020.

Ken P., "An Interview with Stephen Colbert." *IGN.com*, August 11, 2003; updated, May 20, 2012.

Stephanie Kaloi, "Evelyn McGee-Colbert: Stephen Colbert and Evelyn McGee-Colbert have been married since 1993." *People.com*, November 28, 2022.

Tracy Swartz, "Stephen Colbert had a life-changing experience in Chicago that restored his faith in God." *The Chicago Tribune*, November 19, 2018.

Pride or Humility?

Sinful pride pertains to the cravings of our visual perception—not just the tangible things we observe, but also the things we envision or mentally focus on. Additionally, it involves taking excessive pride in our existence, which is often manifested through our tendency to gloat about ourselves and our achievements. Jesus labeled such ostentatious pride as a sin (Mark 7:22), and He, too, faced similar temptations from Satan (Matthew 4:1–11).

Consider the following categories of sinful pride:

- **Pride of birth and rank** (Matthew13:55): "All men are born equal, but quite a few eventually get over it." —Lord Mancroft
- **Pride of wealth** (Matthew 8:20): "I am opposed to millionaires, but it would be dangerous to offer me the position." —Mark Twain
- **Pride of Personal Appearance** (Isaiah 53:2): "It's better to look marvelous than to feel marvelous!" —Billy Crystal
- **Pride of Reputation** (Matthew 11:19): "I am ready to meet my Maker. Whether my Maker is prepared for the ordeal of meeting me is another matter." —Winston Churchill

- **Pride of Success** (Isaiah 53:3): "She always wanted to be successful so she could take it easy. Now she's so successful there's no way she can take it easy." —Unknown
- **Pride of Ability** (John 5:30): "A big head is a big load"—West African saying
- **Pride of Intellect** (John 8:28): "He's very clever, but sometimes his brains go to his head." —Margot Asquith
- **Pride of Self Will** (John 5:30): "Dr. Seuss's first book was rejected by twenty-three publishers."
- **Pride in Death** (Philemon 2:8): "I'm sorry" and "I apologize" mean the same thing. Except at a funeral.

5

PRISM

W hen one tries to describe her, a picture of a prism might come to mind: A solid transparent shape that is bound on all sides by many facets and faces. Spotlights pierce through the prism, illuminating her stage face, flickering across her romantically and disappearing into the shadows of the face on the opposite side, a face that is chipped and hidden from the light. She has a performing face for many and at other times a face that seeks peace and harmony, but in a personal, private way.

***

Keith and Mary were sixteen when they met during the counterculture movement, becoming active participants in the drug scene and partying with rock stars and celebrities. But a divine appointment changed everything. During a 1979 Pat and Buddy Harrison conference, the Lord spoke to them, and their lives were changed forever. That same year, they married, and in 1984 they welcomed their second child, Katheryn Elizabeth, into the world.

GROWING UP POOR BUT "SAFE"

Throughout most of her childhood, Katheryn Elizabeth and her family moved around the country planting churches. Money was tight, and they sometimes relied on their local food bank and food stamps, but they eventually settled in Santa Barbara, California, where Keith and Mary pastored at a Pentecostal church. Their three children Angela, Katheryn Elizabeth, and David attended Christian schools for most of their education

Keith and Mary were very rigid parents. They kept a close eye on what came into their Santa Barbara home, literally keeping the devil from gaining a foothold. They had firsthand knowledge of the undisciplined life and the danger of living a life without purpose, and they wanted to protect their children from it and give them a moral compass. In their home, the Bible was far more than a coffee table book or occasional food for thought. It was lived and walked out wherever they went. They practiced what they preached. Keith and Mary filtered what the children were exposed to. For example, their red canister vacuum was called a "Dirt Angel" instead of Dirt Devil, and they weren't allowed to eat Lucky Charms cereal because that was too much like luck and saying Luc-i-fer. Luck had nothing to do with them. They were "blessed," and that's the word they were to use. Sin, the kids learned, was always at the door. And Mom and Dad were the vigilant guards doing their best to keep it out.

LEAVING THAT 'OL GOSPEL MUSIC

Katheryn Elizabeth basically listened to gospel music, and little else, in the family's home. Christian standards like *Amazing Grace, O Happy Day,* and traditional hymns represented the only music allowed in their home. When she was nine, Katheryn Elizabeth, along with her sister Angela, took voice lessons. When she turned thirteen, Katheryn Elizabeth received a guitar from the church for her birthday. Shortly thereafter, she began writing and performing her own songs, learning by practicing for hours while listening to her older sister's cassette tapes. But it was in church where she became passionate about singing. She could easily change octaves; moving into falsetto and gentle voice, then back to a real strong voice—a move some would consider very difficult vocally.

Because of her parents' rule about secular music, Katheryn Elizabeth was only able to listen to popular music while visiting her friends or smuggling their CDs home. While at a friend's house one day, she heard Alanis Morissette's "You Oughta Know" for the first time. The angry, sexually explicit song struck a chord inside her, changing the direction her singing and songwriting would take.

Sometime later, Katheryn Elizabeth's youth group was witnessing outside a Marilyn Manson concert, handing out "How to Find God" tracts. During the course of the evening, she ventured inside, paused for a moment, then sat down. As she watched the performance, her young eyes were opened to a spectacle she found both strange and fascinating. The longer she watched, the more she felt like something was missing from her own life.

CAREER START

Katheryn Elizabeth completed her GED at the age of sixteen and left school to pursue a career in music. Steve Thomas and Jennifer Knapp recognized her talent and asked her if she'd move to Nashville, Tennessee, to develop her songwriting skills. She jumped at the chance, writing, recording demos, and generally learning more about the business. Red Hill Records signed her and rereleased her debut contemporary Christian album, believing she could be successful. She also began touring with Phil Joel's Strangely Normal Tour, but poor marketing resulted in the tour being financially unsuccessful. Her debut album received mixed reviews, selling only an estimated two hundred copies before the label went out of business. But her journey had only just begun.

Many inspiring songs moved Katheryn Elizabeth at this time, but none moved her more than Freddie Mercury's "Killer Queen." The song unleashed the seventeen-year-old's inventive soul and went on a rampage chasing music's brass ring. It also caused her Pentecostal-shaped world to crumble. The song revealed a lyrical galaxy she never knew existed—about a head-turning, high-class woman entering a room. It pictured something Katheryn Elizabeth had envisioned herself doing one day: commanding everyone's attention.

Of all the globally successful artists in gospel, Christian, Pop or Country music she could have credited with launching her lyrical satellite, she chose Mercury as being the most influential. Deciding to transition from gospel to secular music at the age of seventeen, Katheryn Elizabeth and producer Glen Ballard started to work together. At the same time, she moved to Los Angeles and began music lessons at the Music Academy of the West. In 2004 she signed to Java Records and began working on a solo album, but the project was ultimately scrapped, due to problems between Java Records and its parent company. She then signed with Columbia Records, and by November 2006, she had finished writing and recording what would have been her second studio album. However, before it could be released,

Columbia dropped Katheryn Elizabeth for wanting more control over the production process. She was so close to her album going to full production. Smiling faces, she learned, sometimes told lies.

PERSISTENCE

It was discouraging for Katheryn Elizabeth to be so close to her album's release only to land back at square one. She didn't give up though. Katheryn Elizabeth had learned success would not come easily. She was grateful for the firm foundation her parents had given her. Biblical values formed the foundation of her life, and she knew to always seek God's wisdom and discernment when making a decision. This proved invaluable for navigating the music industry. When Columbia Records dropped her, a sympathetic Columbia publicity executive brought her demos to Virgin Records, where they were convinced she would become a star. In 2007 she signed with Capitol Records and finally released her second studio album in 2008.

It was somewhere in this season of life that Katheryn Elizabeth's moral compass began moving in a direction 180 degrees opposite from the way she had been raised. Katheryn Elizabeth's first single with Capitol Records, "I Kissed a Girl," was the lead single from the album *One of the Boys*. When WRVW aka The River, picked up the song, hundreds called the radio station to complain about its mockery of Christian values, but the song reached number one in the US regardless. Even LGBTQ groups accused the singer of using shock value to sell records.

Queen frontman Freddie Mercury once said excess was a part of his nature and that to him, dullness was a disease and that he needed danger and excitement in his life. Straight people bored him stiff. He loved freaky people. Katheryn Elizabeth's life began to mirror Freddie Mercury's. She was living for pleasure and dead while living. Katheryn Elizabeth began to openly express disdain for Christianity. The sensual nature of her songs increased with her popularity. Her lyrics were increasingly sexually oriented, as were her costumes and dance routines. She openly endorsed the LBGTQ lifestyle in her words, actions, and philanthropy. Her moral compass had all but disappeared.

TAKE-OFF!

Katheryn Elizabeth's career took off with a string of number one hits. She performed all over the world, and made television appearances on *Letterman*, *Saturday Night Live*, and *Sesame Street*, as well as cameos in various film and television series. She coauthored songs recorded by such artists as Kelly

Clarkson, Selena Gomez, Britney Spears, Nicki Minaj, and others.

Katheryn Elizabeth went on to win multiple international music awards and broke records by staying in Billboard's Top 10 for seventeen consecutive months. One album even produced five chart-leading singles—a feat only ever before achieved by Michael Jackson. At one time she had the largest Twitter following in the world.

Before hitting stardom, Katheryn Elizabeth expressed a desire to be successful, yet have a private life. But with grossing $44 million in one year, and fans and paparazzi authenticating every move she made, that was a near impossible objective. Prior to her breakthrough, she had little success and nobody noticed her. Now Katheryn Elizabeth had achieved fame and fortune while commanding the attention of audiences around the world, just as she had dreamed. She was a powerful woman, like the one in Freddie Mercury's song. She was flying high. Fame and fortune were great. She had everything she'd ever dreamed of. Until she didn't.

FALLING

Pride can be harmless when it presents itself as reasonable self-esteem or pleasure derived from a relationship, achievement, or other source of honor. But when allowed to run unchecked, our sin can lead us down paths we never imagined we'd tread, hold us captive longer than we anticipated, and demand a price higher than we ever thought we'd have to pay. Katheryn Elizabeth's pride was flying, but her self-esteem was on a dangerous path.

A two-year relationship failed after she discovered her boyfriend's opioid addiction. Then she married actor Russell Brand, who practiced Hinduism. He and Katheryn Elizabeth skirmished right away. Before they met, the couple had worked hard at their individual crafts. Newly married, neither wanted to abandon what they had worked so hard on to achieve. According to tradition, their Hindu marriage should have lasted seven lifetimes. It only lasted fourteen months. At the end of her marriage, she became distraught and contemplated suicide. However, when the divorce was finalized in 2012, Katheryn Elizabeth began dating guitarist and singer John Mayer, who nicknamed her "Prism."

Speculation grew that her parents were unhappy with her music and career. Her critics were everywhere. One commentator observed that beneath the effortless and catchy tunes of Katheryn Elizabeth, there was an undercurrent of complex emotions. One major Midwest newspaper said her greatest challenge was to be taken seriously. Another newspaper said she was the most important popstar of the day, whose hits everyone related to with little effort. One critic even attacked the sound of her voice. The *Los Angeles Times* took the high road, avoiding any criticism of her voice and music, but they hit a new low faulting her use of idioms, metaphors, and cliches in her lyrics.

In November 2014, Katheryn Elizabeth announced she would perform at the Super Bowl XLIX halftime show. Her provocative, choreographed routines still raised both eyebrows and alarms, but this would be her darkest performance yet.

During halftime in the 2015 National Football League championship game, her production bore a strong resemblance to demonic celebrations. Many visual symbols and imagery associated with Freemasonry and Satanism were presented, prompting alarmed viewers to complain about the satanic ritual they had just witnessed. The sordid show seemed to confirm what she had confessed in an earlier interview: She had sold herself to the devil.

ADULATION AND PRIDE

Like Katheryn Elizabeth's desire for recognition, a problem can develop when we overinvest emotionally in something we are passionate about but neglect to have a life outside that passion. That "something" can, and sadly often does, become the sole source of our self-worth. Then one day that source fails us. It was leading us to a reward we were certain was ours only to have the reward go to someone else we feel is less deserving. We don't get promoted. We don't win the game. Somebody else gets the credit, and we become hurt. We become bitter, and we allow our wounded pride to dictate our life's decisions.

Katheryn Elizabeth's eyes had been laser focused on her public appearances and performances that required constant costume and wardrobe changes, ranging from the sublime to the bizarre. She was constantly concerned with her public persona, the polar opposite of how she was raised.

Katheryn Elizabeth's life began to mirror Freddie Mercury's. She was living for pleasure and dead while living. Flying high above her next record. Fame and fortune were great. She had everything she ever dreamed of. In her mind, she commanded attention from men, women, and children.

Recall the definition of sinful pride includes the desires of "the eyes." This not only pertains to the physical things we observe, but also to the visions we create in our minds. We envision ourselves climbing the corporate ladder, receiving accolades, and basking in applause. Furthermore, pride incorporates the "vanity of life" or sinful yearnings that steer the spotlight towards ourselves. But wealth comes with false promises. Katheryn Elizabeth hung her entire self-worth on the success of her career, and when her fifth album didn't do as well as her previous ones, she slipped into a dark depression.

Katheryn Elizabeth described feeling caught between two personas—that of a pop superstar and the private person embodied by her family. How she perceived herself was taking a toll. Seeing her career spiral hit her hard, breaking her spirit in half. She realized she didn't have a clear direction for her life. Her bent toward religious pluralism, mixed with her own interpretation of the Bible, led to bouts of alcoholism, depression, anxiety, and thoughts of suicide. She didn't want to leave her bed. She couldn't face seeing anyone or doing anything.

CHOOSE HUMILITY OR PRIDE

After hitting this dark point in her life, Katheryn Elizabeth said she had to work on her mental health. She was determined to make some changes. Through therapy, the eyes of her heart were opened. She could see in her brokenness that her life actually had a purpose. Her self-worth was not defined by fame, wealth, record sales, and "likes" on social media. She could feel whole by living a humble life with purpose rather than living like a popstar all the time. The remedy called for her to begin a daily regimen of expressing gratitude. The practice saved her life. Without it, she believed she would have continued down the dark path before her.

Through joint counseling, Katheryn Elizabeth and her family have healed and grown closer. The sessions also helped her remember her Christian foundation. God had created her for a purpose. She was not disposable. She remembered that God does not call the equipped, He equips the called and those willing to serve Him. Katheryn Elizabeth confesses to praying all the time for self-control and for humility, knowing God resists the proud but gives grace to the humble. After navigating depression and anxiety for years, her eyes are once again full of light, and she has a positive outlook on life.

> "Your eye is like a lamp that provides light for your body. When your eye is healthy, your whole body is filled with light. But when your eye is unhealthy, your whole body is filled with darkness"
> (Matthew 6:22–23).

Katheryn Elizabeth's career also picked up when she was asked to be a judge on *American Idol*, for which she happily signed a $25M contract.

HAPPIER DAYS

Early on, Katheryn Katheryn Elizabeth Hudson realized a need to perform under a different name. Her family called her Katy, so her first album was simply *Katy Hudson*. But she realized she might get confused with an actress with a similar name. So, she made a strategic decision. She adopted her mother's maiden name of Perry and made the transition to superstar Katy Perry.

In 2019, Katy Perry got engaged to English actor Orlando Bloom, and a year later, she gave birth to their daughter, Daisy Dove. An incredible transition from pop superstar to superstar mom and wife had begun. Becoming a mother was the exact change Katy Perry's life needed. Having Daisy changed her priorities and perspective on life, brought her life into balance, and gave it real meaning—something the artificial world of Hollywood never could. Katy described being a mom as a real shift, but the best one.

The fervent prayers of Katy's family were powerful in their effect. She knew her mother had prayed for her all her life, hoping she would return back to God. But in her mind, Katy never left Him. She was just a tad lost, materialistic, and career driven.

RESOURCES

Geoffrey Grider, "Former Christian Singer Katy Perry Admits She Sold Her Soul To The Devil And Doesn't Try To Hide It Now." *Now the End Begins*, February 27, 2015.

Theendbegins.com/katy-perry-admits-sold-soul-devil-video.

Matthew Trzcinski, "How a Queen Song About a Prostitute Inspired Katy Perry's Career." *Cheatsheet.com,* March 26, 2020.

Michael Cragg, "I created this character called Katy Perry. I didn't want to be Katheryn Hudson. It was too scary." Interview. *The Guardian,* June 11, 2017.

Phoebe Loomes, "Katy Perry's strange path to fame. Raised by hippies; turned born-again Christian, denied access to education, Katy Perry's path to fame was stranger than fiction." *News.com,* September 22, 2018.

Sam Murphy, "The Rapid Rise And Awkward Fall Of Katy Perry." *Junkies.com,* n.d.

Shirley Halperin, "Katy Perry: Confessions of a Pop Princess. Updated: The purple-haired sexpot spills tears and secrets in her concert film, 'Part of Me,' as the one-time religious teen one-ups even studio execs with her power." *The Hollywood Reporter, Plus Icon,* June 20, 2012.

Toyin Owoseje, "Katy Perry says she felt suicidal during split from Orlando Bloom." *CNN.com,* June 29, 2020.

ABANDON THE GOD OF YOUR YOUTH?

When we abandon the God of our youth, we often experience a profound shift in our perspective and worldview. This abandonment can be a result of disillusionment, personal growth, or exposure to new ideas and beliefs. It's a process that is usually accompanied by a period of questioning and introspection. We start to reevaluate the principles and values that were once integral to our identity. This can lead to feelings of confusion, fear, and even guilt, especially if our former faith was a significant part of our upbringing and community.

You might think that leaving behind the God of your youth can be a liberating experience and believe the lie that ignoring God allows you to explore other spiritual paths and philosophies, broadening your understanding of the world and your place in it. But when you grow away from God's boundaries and are arrogant enough to believe you can define your own beliefs rather than accepting those in the Bible, your questions, doubts, and truth-seeking will never lead you to the one true God you're looking for.

You will feel a sense of loss and go through a mourning period for the comfort and certainty that faith once provided. Relationships may change as well, particularly with those who still follow Jesus.

You may feel a sense of isolation away from the family of believers God gave you. Come back to the Lord. Return to your church or seek out a new faith-filled community and form new connections based on your childhood faith. Don't experience the long-term consequences of sinful pride and return to the Father's arms, where you will only experience grace and forgiveness, along with a restored life purpose.

6

BUCK

Toph was a private pilot and a good one. Twice he flew solo across the Atlantic. But flying a plane would not be how the world would come to know him. His ancestors had also crossed the Atlantic as early as the 1600s. Some on the Mayflower. Still others from the French aristocracy. His family thought he was out of this world. And they were not alone. Toph was an all-American who would be one of the best-known names in film, but as he lay on the ground, unable to move, he knew his career was over.

***

Toph's father, Frank, grew up in a wealthy family but became estranged from them and their riches. After graduating from Princeton and marrying Barbara, Frank's English degree and love of Russian literature didn't pay for much. Despite living in a low-rent place on the Upper East Side, making ends meet was a challenge.

About a year into the marriage, Barbara gave birth to Toph, a boy with a splash of blond hair and blue eyes. The happy parents wasted no time growing their family, with Benjamin born a year later. They were a difficult few years, with a convergence of unmet needs making the atmosphere at home difficult.

Their stormy home drew Toph and Ben closer together. In their precious imaginations, they escaped through play, creating their pre-K version of *Live at the Improv*. They employed cardboard boxes that once carried groceries and bottles that once carried milk. Nothing was off the table. Yet they could not help hearing their parents' angry charges, lobbed grenade-like at one another most of the time. Eventually, his parents quit.

Like so many children of divorce, Toph felt torn between them. They used him as a chess piece. Game. Set. Match. Barbara moved to a college town in Mercer County with the boys. She had custody, but Frank had visitation rights, which he was good about following. Barbara worked as a journalist for the local newspaper, working her way up to editor. Frank remarried and lived in New York, and like a kid on restriction, Frank could not afford to travel far from campus. Even if he had money, he didn't have the time beyond weekends to visit the boys. For Toph and Ben, life quickly become complex.

A New Family

Their mom began dating and eventually married Tristam, a financially successful stockbroker who created a new lifestyle for the two boys in which they didn't have to watch every penny. But with this upgrade in living came the peculiarity of a blended, ready-made family with two younger stepbrothers, Mark and Brock, Tristam's kids.

Tristam was generous and emotionally connected to his children. He not only embraced the role of stepfather, but he also loved Toph and Ben just like his own. Their new home was also filled with laughter, a welcome change for the two boys. Tristam enrolled them at Princeton Day School, where they maximized their academic potential, receiving an excellent college prep education. But there was one thing Tristam absolutely would not allow in the house—a television. The kids were to use their free time doing more productive things.

The gauntlet of the past, though, had left its mark on Toph, filling him with the need to be successful on his own—independent and not a team player, able to stand out, to be the very best at anything he took on. He got his dad's attention and pleased him at the same time. It was a win-win. In spite of everything, Toph still looked up to his father. Frank had achieved a lot and done it without anyone's help.

Not even God's. The only way Toph could live up to that was to win at all cost.

HIS GIFTS MADE A WAY

Toph was gifted musically. He sang soprano with the school madrigal group and demonstrated a talent for piano. "When you play, never mind who listens to you," said composer Robert Schumann. So Toph practiced alone, and it brought him great peace. Toph wasn't just a Renaissance man, he fenced and played hockey, but otherwise generally avoided team sports. He never got too close to anyone, so that if they ever left him, he wouldn't end up emotionally broken.

It wasn't until he was invited to audition for a singing role in a production of Gilbert and Sullivan's *The Yeoman of the Guard* that he even considered acting. He didn't know what he was getting into. He'd need to learn how to adapt into any kind of character. He didn't wait too long to share his newfound taste for acting with his family and his dad. The genre fitted him perfectly, and he found that it helped him loosen up and relax.

Performing, Toph discovered, provided an escape route from things he was not prepared to deal with. Outwardly, everything seemed just fine. He had food, clothing, shelter, a quality education, and more. Internally, scars from his family's breakup dampened any desire to mingle outside his routine. Toph's passion for the performing arts did not go unnoticed by his mom and Trist. They were behind him 100 percent, doing all they could to encourage him. But the people at the McCarter Theater played an even larger role in Toph's development as a young man. Around them he learned to think for himself.

COLLEGE CALLS

After graduating from high school, Toph performed in a few plays locally, with the intention of starting a career in theater in New York. His wise mother advised him to go to college first, so he chose Cornell University, and he promised his mother and stepfather he'd finish college before pursuing acting full time.

Sin is always at the door. Late in his freshman year, Toph was approached by a well-known talent manager who wanted to represent him. The stagestruck Toph could not contain himself, repeatedly reading the letter. In his excitement, Toph didn't realize the invitation was a test of sorts. Satan knows our weaknesses. Impatience and the pace of school were Toph's. He took a bite out of the forbidden fruit and met with the agent, considering breaking his promise to his parents. But to his chagrin, the agent encouraged him to stay in college. To keep the stage lights on in the student actor's life, though, the agent set up a program where Toph was introduced to various casting agents and producers he could work for during his upcoming summer vacation. Toph found each introduction and audition productive and received positive feedback. But the enemy doesn't give up. Toph was tempted again with offers. But their schedules conflicted with his college courses and he had to turn them down. That summer he toured in a production of *Forty Carats*, and the following year, Toph worked in the San Diego Shakespeare Festival.

Though his acting career was in play, a hunger remained to know more about his ancestry, about the landscape the family cultivated. So, before his junior year, Toph flew to the UK to watch a number of productions in Scotland, England, and Wales. He spent time with the actors, too, asking questions about stage life and even helping them with their American accents. Weeks later, he studied French theater in Paris, where he forced himself to speak only French. He had learned the language beginning in third grade through his freshman year at Cornell but had never been challenged to speak it.

Back on US soil, Toph focused on acting and little else, but he had yet to complete all the requirements for graduation from Cornell. So, he was encouraged to transfer as a theater major to Juilliard—an incredibly difficult school to get into. Toph's audition caused Academy Award-winner

John Houseman to offer Toph a spot in the Acting Company. But Toph declined, keeping his promise to get his bachelor's degree after moving to Juilliard.

Toph, along with his peers from Juilliard, embarked on a tour across New York City's middle schools, performing *The Love Cure*. In one unforgettable act, Toph, in the role of the protagonist, swung his sword too high, inadvertently smashing a line of lights overhead. This unexpected incident was something only his classmate Robin Williams could truly appreciate. The audience erupted into such cheers and applause, Toph later said it was the loudest ovation he had ever received in his career. Upon finishing at Juilliard, Toph achieved his Bachelor of Arts degree.

In many ways Toph was like his father. Tall. Handsome. Charismatic. But his relationship with Frank was difficult. Frank's love for his children seemed predicated on performance. To gain his father's approval, Toph pressured himself to act older than he actually was. Frank avoided church and had no use for religion. When he drove Toph and Ben home or to the train station on Sundays, he made disparaging comments about people coming out of worship services. He called them sheep, and Toph would immediately agree.

Throughout much of his life, Toph considered himself an atheist. Frank spoke multiple languages, but for seven years they barely spoke to each other.

It was a bridge too far. But one day tragedy would lead them to meet each other halfway.

OPPORTUNITY

Neil Armstrong and Buzz Aldrin had walked on the moon years before Academy Award-winning Katharine Hepburn cast Toph in the play *A Matter of Gravity*. But there was a conflict. Toph was already in the CBS television soap opera *Love of Life*. Hepburn intervened and persuaded the network to work with Toph to reconcile the schedule conflicts between *Love of Life* and *Gravity* so he could do both.

Jesus said that man cannot live on bread alone. Toph was making lots of bread, but his full schedule left little time to eat any of the sandwich variety, much less rest. Candy bars and coffee were poor substitutes. Exhaustion and malnutrition played the leading roles. The combination was like kryptonite to Superman. During the debut night of the play, Toph stepped onto the stage, delivered his inaugural line, and promptly collapsed—an unscripted act. Hepburn, famous for playing John Wayne's love interest in *The Quiet Man*, addressed the audience, announcing Toph was foolish and that he didn't eat enough red meat. Subsequently, the understudy took over and completed the performance. Eventually, Toph recovered, sought help, and performed the role until the play ended.

Toph wanted more. He wanted challenging, interesting parts. Not satisfied with television and theater, he took on the role of Lieutenant (JG) Phillips in *Gray Lady Down*. This debut film performance led to more film opportunities like *The Remains of the Day*.

Toph became a family man. Now married with children, he worked hard to make sure his kids lived a normal life far from the artificial Hollywood world. Instead, his children had a regular upbringing in the New York suburbs of school, homework, and firm rules. His stepfather had been a good role model.

HIS BIG BREAKTHROUGH

Toph had made certain his headshot was on file with the Screen Actors Guild so casting directors could find him. Sure enough, his agent informed him he'd set up a meeting with the producer and director of a much-advertised film. Toph wasn't exactly thrilled with the idea of making a film from an illustrated story, even when told he was in the running for the lead role. But a basic tenet of acting, especially when looking for work, is to never turn down an appointment. So, he went, even though he doubted he would get the part. Toph's photo had been singled out from the union files by the film's casting director, who liked his look and résumé. But live and in-person, Toph clashed with the ideal. He was 6'4" but scrawny. He had black hair and blue eyes but a baby face. Yet, his resemblance to the illustrated story's hero was close enough that the producer and director felt a reading of the script was warranted.

Things really took off when they asked him to put on a pair of glasses and read a different script. The metamorphosis was obvious as Toph shaped himself into a totally different person. They were stunned by what they saw. Before he knew it, Toph was on the next flight to London for a screen test. When he got the news, he called his mom and Tristam. Ben was next. Then his half-sister Allison. And everyone around the world would hear it soon too.

It was the start of 1977 when Toph signed his contract. Unfortunately, there wasn't much money left over for the star. Chris Nickson, in his biography about Toph, said the contract called for him to receive $250,000 a year, including the years filming the sequel. He would be paid $5,000 a week for work beyond that. It was an offer he couldn't refuse.

To prepare for the role, Toph required a considerable physical transformation. He'd worn a padded costume for the screen test, but the filming required much more. He was tall and lanky and needed to add thirty pounds of muscle to the nearly two hundred he was already carrying. He began eating four meals a day and lifting weights three hours daily, with the finished goal of wide shoulders and no waist.

With only three months before filming, Toph made the most of his time. When he wasn't working out, he prepared for the dual roles. He acquired old suits, bought glasses, and made sure Clark Kent and Superman would have completely different makeup. His disciplined life of physical training and role preparation provided a pathway to effectively portray the character. His approach was to recognize the importance of humanizing Superman.

The American premiere took place in Washington, D.C.. The film's debut in Britain, though technically "public," was in reality a private screening before Queen Elizabeth II and other guests. When theatergoers saw Toph as both Clark Kent and Superman in the opening scenes, they were speechless. But in the scenes that followed, it was his acting ability that kept them glued to their seats. Huge ticket sales motivated the producers to plan even more sequels.

Like lobby cards, the story of how *Superman* came to be was split into three parts. First, as predicted by the respected scientist Jor-El, the fictional planet Krypton was destroyed. Jor-El sent Kal-El, his only son and the only survivor of his race, to Smallville, Earth. This introduced the audience to the young Clark Kent and Ma and Pa Kent who raised him. The film transitioned to the third phase when Clark graduated from high school. Then followed the sequels—*Superman II,* which was Toph's favorite of the series; *Superman III*, released in 1983; followed by the 1997 release of *Superman IV: The Quest for Peace*.

It wasn't his superpowers that made Superman a hero. It was understanding that Superman had been supernaturally gifted to serve others in humility. Toph became a philanthropist, visited terminally ill children through the Make-A-Wish Foundation, and served on the board of directors for Save the Children.

Toph was born into a Presbyterian church family. Presbyterians believe in the sovereignty of God, salvation through grace, and the authority of Scripture. But once Toph embarked on his career, he stopped going to church and lived an atheistic life. He didn't believe he needed God.

SUBSEQUENT ROLES

With *Superman* over, Toph's next movie *Somewhere in Time* was a commercial failure and Toph's first public disappointment. In the next decade, Toph starred in *Street Smart*, *The Rose and the Jackal*, and *The Remains of the Day*. The latter film was nominated for eight Academy Awards.

Toph was now getting plenty of work. He no longer had trouble making ends meet. The *Superman* films were a large deposit on long-time financial security for him and his family. But he was dissatisfied with the roles he was getting. He was always wanting to expand his acting ability. Superman wasn't an idol. Acting was, and he was getting prideful because he felt he had accomplished his success all by himself.

"It is sin to know what you ought to do and then not do it" (James 4:17).

In a 1988 interview with Larry King, Toph admitted to not believing in God or even a higher power. He kept thinking he was the author of his destiny.

PREPARING FOR ROLES

Toph accepted the role of a paralyzed police officer in the movie *Above Suspicion*. He prepared for the role at a Californian rehab facility, where he learned how to transition from a wheelchair to a mattress and into a car. While Toph trained in the therapy room, he frequently saw a woman who had been crushed under a bookshelf during a disaster. In his memoir, *Still Me,* Toph saw that she wore a halo attached to her head as she learned to walk again. He noticed how deeply depressed she was, struggling with the reality of her condition. Pridefully, the world's Superman said he tried to conceal his emotions as he watched her struggling to take small, agonizing steps forward, holding herself up on the parallel bars.

In the field and power of his x-ray vision, the story of the good Samaritan had unfolded. He had the power, authority, and responsibility to help. The character he portrayed had been supernaturally gifted to help others. Yet, Toph did nothing. His pride of position led him to walk on by. At the end of each practice session, Toph retreated to the comforts of the Sunset Marquis Hotel, thinking all the while *Thank God that's not me.* He had no idea what was coming. About a year later, in 1995, *Above Suspicion* premiered. The film received mixed reviews, but Toph's performance, in general, was well received.

Toph started horse-riding, overcoming allergies to horse hair, to the point when he began entering competitions on his twelve-year-old American thoroughbred nicknamed "Buck." At the same time, he was acting in the satanic film *Village of the Damned.* The science fiction film is about a small British village where, after a mysterious blackout, women give birth to unfriendly alien children posing as humans. Unknown to Tosh, this would be the last publicly released film he would star in.

IT ALL COMES CRASHING DOWN

In between projects, Toph trained with Buck and entered training level events, making plans to move up to preliminary level in 1996. Although Toph had entered a competition in Vermont, his coach encouraged him to go to Culpepper, Virginia, instead, to participate in a dressage and combined training finals at an equestrian center.

On Memorial Day 1995, Toph was in the top four in the dressage, but on his cross-country portion of the competition, Buck refused at the third jump—a routine jump over a 3" fence shaped like the letter W. Toph fell off the horse, landing headfirst in a way that broke his neck and instantly paralyzed him from the neck down. He was medevacked to Charlottesville and the University of Virginia Medical Center. Inside the emergency room, attendants secured his personal property, including a neck chain with a pendant. On the pendant was a single word, "faith."

RECONSIDERING ETERNITY

It wasn't until after the Culpepper accident that Toph reevaluated where he might spend eternity. Thoughts of suicide crossed his mind—he didn't want to be a burden to his wife and family. But wife Dana assured him that he had much to live for, including her. They didn't know what the future held, and Toph finally accepting his inability to rule his own life, felt a need to be spiritual. To this end he eventually joined the Unitarian Universalist Church. The organization's spiritual platform welcomes everyone who is free to believe what they want. He could write his own script about eternity and his own definition of heaven. It was just what he wanted. It was *not* what he needed.

Everyone else called him Toph, but his wife always called him Chris. When the family was together, everyone heard his given name: Chris-Toph-er. Christopher Reeve had once played the Man of Steel who could see through walls, but he had pridefully erected walls of intellect around his heart and soul. His pride was his kryptonite, spiritually blinding him, preventing him from seeing the truth that would set him free. Sadly, he died not knowing his eternal destination. It was right in front of him the whole time.

RESOURCES

Chris Nickson, *A Biography of Christopher Reeve*. New York: St. Martin's Paperbacks, 1998.

Christell Fatima M. Tudtud, "Christopher Reeve aka 'Superman' Never Believed in God & Once Admitted He Didn't Pray." *News.amomama.com*, Nov 14, 2021.

Christopher Reeve, *Still Me*. New York: Random House, 1998.

Christopher and Dana Reeve Foundation: Christopherreeve.org/blog/daily-dose/a-single-centimeter-a-ruined-life-the-accident-that-caused-christopher-reeve-superman-to-go-from-a-star-to-legend.

"The Gospel According to Christopher Reeve—Unitarian Universalism." *Market Faith.org*, n.d..

Lynn Eaton, "C. Reeve: Man and Superman," Interview. *BMJ*, June 14, 2003: 326(7402):1287-90. doi: 10.1136/bmj.326.7402.1287. PMID: 12805155; PMCID: PMC1126178.

SINFUL PRIDE IS KRYPTONITE

Why is sinful pride a man's kryptonite? Before we look at the answer, let's review some basic comic book history about this made-up mineral. According to the Superman stories, Kryptonite is a green, glassy material found on the fictional planet Krypton. Kryptonite is the name given to shards of matter cast off from the planet during its destruction. When Superman is exposed to Kryptonite, he loses his superpowers, is weakened, and can die. Like kryptonite to Superman, sinful pride attacks our desire to resist sin.

Pride and lust are like kryptonite for the mind. Pride can lead us to very dark places and drag us through experiences we never wanted, just like Samson (of the Bible) experienced.

SAMSON AND DALILAH

When Samson messed around with Delilah, he never imagined that their unhealthy relationship would be so talked about three thousand years later. Samson's strength—he was often called the strongest man to ever live—came from God alone, and Samson knew he was just a vessel used by God to display His strength.

Despite being born with extraordinary potential, Samson squandered his life due to sin. This serves as a vital lesson for us; the more we let ourselves be seduced by the deceptive allure of sin, the more our spiritual vision is obscured. Before he was physically blinded, Samson had already lost his spiritual sight by involving himself with a woman he had been divinely warned to avoid (Judges 14:3). We must acknowledge the truth that sin has the power to infiltrate our lives, causing blindness and desensitization. If we don't actively resist it, we can easily find ourselves entrapped by it, much like Samson.

Every sin carries with it serious and sometimes fatal repercussions. Sin first ensnares us, then it obscures our vision, and eventually it wears us down (Judges 16:21). In reality, sin can lead us further astray than we ever intended to wander. It can detain us for longer than we planned to linger. Moreover, the price we pay for sin is often more than we ever expected to bear. We must heed the stern admonition to "guard your heart above all else, for it determines the course of your life" (Proverbs 4:23).

God employs both the wicked and the righteous to fulfill His divine purpose. We learn that neither our righteousness nor our wickedness can obstruct God's will. While God does punish wrongdoing, He may delay the execution of judgment. Samson was a superficial and vindictive man who sulked when things didn't go his way. His statements about the Philistines are particularly revealing: "Samson said,

'This time I cannot be blamed for everything I am going to do ... I only did to them what they did to me" (Judges 15: 3, 11). In seeking revenge, he met his end alongside the very men he considered himself superior to.

The truth is that had Samson obeyed God throughout his life, he never would have ended up dead under the weight of the temple he was mocked in. The same goes for us. We must always trust God and obey Him, no matter what.

7

YOU'RE FIRED

He was losing energy at the same time his debt was surging. The power in his house had been cut off. His family was facing foreclosure. His wife had left him for good. His only interest was in drugs. Even he didn't think he would make it out alive.

***

Wilmar was raised in Twin Cities by his single mother. His parents had divorced when he was in second grade. As the eldest, Wilmar was no stranger to bearing a hefty load of responsibilities. However, navigating a new city, a new school, and unfamiliar faces was a different ballgame altogether. Eager to blend in, he became a magnet for attention, resorting to outrageous antics as a diversionary tactic from potential bullying. For example one day, when the bus was only a few blocks from school, he decided to respond to a double-dog dare. Always acting first, thinking later, a snowbank up ahead seemed to call out "Jump!" A great leap of faith was an instinct away. If he played his cards right, he would hit big and land safely.

He lowered the top pane of the window and was hanging outside. His hands—from the outside-in—held a death grip on the window frame. He'd gone out feet first. The Twin-Cities wind pummeled his blue parka, rushing around his hood. With his feet firmly planted against the bus's yellow skin, he surveyed the snowbank-lined street ahead. By now the bullies from fifth grade had crowded around Wilmar's vacated seat, waiting for him to lunge from the moving bus. Down the street Chaska Elementary loomed larger and larger. He had to make a move. Cold and alone, he was literally an outsider. And had no idea where he would land . . . He twisted in midair, arching his body toward the snowbank and landing with a *plumph* into a giant pillow of powdery white snow. The reception he got from the school principal wasn't nearly as soft.

This kind of behavior became increasingly common, leading Wilmar to take more and more risks, eventually leading him to gambling, which began to emerge in his teenage years.

> *"We make our decisions and then our decisions turn around and make us."*
> —F. W. Boreham

COLLEGE YEARS

Upon completing high school, Wilmar secured a spot at the University of Minnesota. However, he soon discovered a profound disinterest in academic pursuits. Balancing two jobs, one at a drive-in cinema and the other at a grocery store, he struggled to adhere to the rules. After being dismissed from multiple positions, he distinctly recalls the grocery store owner suggesting he should start his own company, hinting at what the future had in store for him.

Wilmar's challenges weren't limited to maintaining employment; he also lacked the motivation to attend lectures, only showing up once or twice a semester. He experienced intense envy as he watched his peers graduate from college and build successful careers with the same companies they'd been with since high school. In contrast, Wilmar felt like he was stuck on a merry-go-round, making no progress in life. The habit of comparing himself to others led to feelings of inadequacy and low self-esteem. To numb this emotional pain, he sought solace in alcohol and drugs.

ADDICTIONS

Without a job and not attending class, Wilmar's drinking quickly got out of control, leading to numerous tickets and several DWIs. He was escaping reality, but drinking wasn't enough.

Cocaine changed everything. He was instantly hooked. Cocaine gave Wilmar a feeling that he found hard to describe. It made him feel like he could go where he wanted without alcohol and still function. Cocaine was an escape. He quickly became a high-functioning addict. Wilmar was also incurring gambling debts.

One summer Wilmar got a job on a relative's farm. But it was hard work. He worked for six months, returning back home most every night to be with his bar buds and party with them. But he felt deep shame about his position in life, and it surfaced at his high school reunion five years after graduating, where his peers talked about all the great things they had achieved in that time. The lives of people he'd known since high school had entered the fast lane and passed him by. They seemed to have it all together. Not Wilmar. He was basically the same as the day they'd left high school. Only worse. He no longer even had the job at the *Flying Cloud* drive-in movie theater or the job at the grocery store.

GAMBLING

The reunion had been an eye opener for Wilmar but a downer at the same time. He was met with more turmoil and trouble. When this happened, he responded like any other addict. He took to another means of escape: sports betting. He was a compulsive gambler—in over his head in debt with some ruthless people after him all the time. Chronologically he was in his mid-twenties. But he had the emotional maturity of a kid who happened to owe $20,000.

CHASED BY THE MOB

When we're knee-deep in sin, things will always get out of control. That's why siblings share secret codes—to subtly alert the other that they are in immediate danger without tipping off the enemy. For example, a brother could ask "How are things at the shop?" The sibling in peril would reply, "Like witches' brew." Translation: I'm in trouble.

That's the way it was for Wilmar. He was in witches' brew trouble. He feared for his life. While working at a neighborhood grocery store, he told a coworker one day that he owed the mob $20,000. If anyone should come in looking like they were collecting money, he wanted his coworker to announce over the store intercom that Wilmar had a telephone call on "Line 3." Since the store only had two lines, that was his code that the people he was afraid of were in the store and to run. Later that day, the plan worked to perfection. But he couldn't avoid the bookies forever. Eventually Wilmar paid off his $20,000 debt, but not before turning over everything he had, including his trailer.

Wilmar's gambling addiction was no different than that of other compulsive gamblers. Most do not just gamble on one type of athletic contest, game of chance, cards, horserace, or sport. Wilmar had a particular fondness for card games, blackjack being his favorite. His obsession was so intense that he even enrolled in a six-month course taught by a renowned card guru in Minneapolis to learn card counting. This newly acquired skill set him on a path to Las Vegas, where he planned to outsmart the casinos and settle his debts with the bookies he invariably found himself indebted to.

Drivers in snow country are encouraged to stay behind the snowplow to stay alive. The trouble was Wilmar's snowplow was a straw over a line of cocaine. He was always behind—constantly in debt, incurring huge gambling losses, and getting high. But he would find ways to get money, stay operational, and keep the bookmakers happy.

LIVING BUT DYING

The year had been a banner one, and Wilmar went to Las Vegas to feed off chips, nuts, and other bar snacks while living out of his van, gambling so he could win enough to pay off his debts. He stayed dry the entire time, not because he wanted to be clean but to have a clear head. He was in a desperate situation, and drinking alcohol was a storm drain to winning. He focused on winning. He would walk away with the $350 or so he won every night and send it home to his mom. She settled with the bookies and also made installment payments toward past-due bank loans.

Wilmar's risky lifestyle didn't allow for what he wanted: a family. He prayed that one day he would be married and have children. A popular song once advised against looking too hard but waiting too long for the right girl. About the time Wilmar met her, he reckoned she was "the one." He was smitten, and two years later they married. But things did not turn out the way he'd hoped. Like gambling, he'd taken a chance on love. The harder he tried, the more he lost.

HIS AVOIDANCE CONTINUES

Wilmar left work drunk one evening, driving into a snowstorm, and he rolled his car on Highway 41. Ironically it was near the same spot where he'd jumped out of the school bus window in the fifth grade, but this time he had cracked ribs and worse—another DUI. Within a week he had another run-in with the police. Facing serious jail time, he checked himself into the regional drug treatment center.

But even in rehab, he continued plying the tricks of the trade. Addicts conversationally are like flimflam men, using a polished sales pitch to dupe family, the elderly, and the woefully ignorant out of their savings. They persuade them to give, lend money, or otherwise support schemes the junkies are involved in. They're conniving and often won't take no for an answer.

Wilmar's goal wasn't to get sober and clean. His agenda was to get the "Tif," a sheet of paper to show the court that he had completed a thirty-day, residential, substance abuse treatment program. He hoped the certificate would convince a judge not to send him to jail. He played the game.

In group and individual sessions, Wilmar rejected the program's guilt therapy-based approach. Interventions included questions designed to get the self-centered addict to switch their attitude to acknowledging the pain and suffering inflicted on friends and family. "Do you know how upset they are? They've been hurt by your addictions. Have you added up all the money you've blown on drugs?" He knew, he would say. Then apologize. I'm so sorry. He knew what to say to please the counselors.

Inwardly, he mocked the process. Did the counselors really believe leading along this path would make him drug free? Others' suffering was the furthest thing from his mind. He rationalized his behavior and blamed others for his problems. Admitting he had wounded his family and others, and acknowledging that was why he was broke, made him want to do drugs even more. Speaking *that* truth wasn't going to get him a *Get Out of Jail Free* card.

Fine-tuning his responses and feigning humility, he apologized and promised to change.

The approach did little to suppress Wilmar's desire for alcohol, gambling, or drugs. From where he sat, those were the only things that would boost his attitude. He was so lost, he didn't know of any other way to live. What hurt was that people knew where he was, yet no one reached out to him.

One night he found he couldn't sleep, so he stared at the TV, watching a guy from out west who ran a food truck. He sold sandwiches and beverages to people at local companies between hanging out at the beach. Wilmar was intrigued. Would this work for him?

HOPE?

Wilmar got right to work in developing a business plan, letting it become his newest obsession. He played the recovery game even harder than before. He wanted to get out as soon as possible and put the food truck business in gear. He complied with all the directions from counselors and other staff. Almost. On his ward, he ran nickel-and-dime gambling games. Day after day he improved his con of the counselors. Twenty-eight days into the program, he was released.

Free at last, Wilmar brought the plan up to speed. With a friend and the friend's $8,000, a used food truck was purchased. Just like that, Sunshine Concessions had wheels. Wilmar's business model was centered on marketing to employees in the Chaska Industrial Park all the way to Chanhassen, but he needed permission to operate, and he got turned down numerous times. But he didn't stop trying.

THE WINDS OF CHANGE

Wilmar's fortunes turned when he managed to meet with the president of a very large company. He wanted to help Wilmar, but preexisting vendors and other agreements took precedent. But Wilmar would not take no for an answer. He threw the dice. If he was given permission to operate, he offered to give each of the company's employees a free sandwich at lunch every day for one business week. The president was impressed by the offer but still had reservations. But Wilmar would not give up. He overcame each objection the executive had, and thirty minutes later, Wilmar had his authorization. Getting the account produced a high he'd never experienced before, and it was not likely one he'd ever forget.

His partner thought the deal was crazy, but Wilmar saw it differently. He believed that when employees came to get their free sandwich, they would buy chips, drinks, cookies, candy, and fruit pies to go with them. He was right.

A NEW DEAL

So it was with a small bar and nightclub Wilmar wanted to buy, but he couldn't get a loan on his own. So off the charts was his credit reputation, he even got turned down for a library card. But he was able to talk friends and family into buying the business for him. In return, he would pay them back, and he would own the entities outright. The plan was brilliant. Use *their* money and financial reputation.

Schmitty's—a place where everyone knows your name—now belonged to Wilmar. His idea was to create a bar where everyone felt welcome—from bikers to construction workers. And he succeeded. He was more than an owner. He was involved, managing the operation from mid-morning until the early morning hours.

In business there's a profit and a loss. Wilmar profited by being at work, where he had to pay bills, supervise, and develop a diverse customer base. But there were major losses on his children's activities and on his marriage. He invested time and energy in the business while shortchanging his wife and family. And *that* was a crime. Spending time at Schmitty's provided great cover for the monkey that was on Wilmar's back. There was no separation. His addictions went everywhere he went. Keeping up with them was hard work. Wilmar was always away from home, in the vicious cycle of hiding, lying, and feeding his addictions.

Wilmar's cycle of addiction went something like this: he would be at a party and getting ready to leave and indicate he going home. But homeward bound he wasn't. The story he dropped would give him cover while simultaneously feeding the addiction, like creating excuses for going somewhere or being late—details that were hard to remember and cover. This was the world Wilmar inhabited. Being a bar owner conveniently provided a facade for his vices. The late nights out were justified as "work," and any questionable activities could be brushed off under the pretense of being in the hospitality industry.

The demanding hours of operating Schmitty's spilled over into the community. Like softball. Wilmar didn't just sponsor softball teams, he built leagues for men and women. Wilmar wore more hats at softball games than Sheriff Andy Taylor. Softball became a new crutch, like the other addictions. He simply could not delegate responsibility. It was he who took care of the fields. It was he who turned off the stadium lights. He even umpired games.

Leveling Up

Wilmar was ready to take his bar business to the next level. A friend from Kansas City had expressed a desire to partner with him in the purchase of two other bars: Suds and Someplace Else. Wilmar would manage the bars while the partner and one other investor would remain behind the scenes. It was an intriguing opportunity, but it required an infusion of significant cash that Wilmar clearly did not have. So, he contacted a man who had a successful medical supply business and a second man who was a potential investor. Wilmar was adept at reading other gamblers, but he couldn't get a good read on these men. Ignoring his gut feelings, he sold them 38 percent of the initial stock offering. With new cash, the company expanded, and Wilmar and his wife became salaried employees. They would also maintain control of the company. The basic arrangement meant Wilmar and his family would, for the first time in their marriage, have steady income and not live show to show any longer.

State tax law required the creation of a board of directors. The two major investors expressed a desire to be on it and Wilmar agreed. Part of Wilmar felt good about the new arrangement. But a nagging subtle uneasiness was there too. *What's wrong with this picture?*

They smiled in his face, but unknown to him, they purchased an additional 3 percent of company stock from other investors, giving them a controlling interest. The board of director rules said stockholders with 60 percent ownership could vote members off the board. At the end of a December shareholders meeting, everyone had left except for Wilmar, his brother, and the two investors. Looking across the table they said to Wilmar, "Good meeting. By the way, you're fired."

Leaving and Going Back to Las Vegas

When Wilmar left Las Vegas, he swore he would never play blackjack again. He kept that promise for about twenty years before Wilmar told his son the story. He had broken the rules of the card-counting game, he confessed, and gotten kicked out of casinos. His son asked him why he couldn't go back and do it right this time. The devil will always make sin sound attractive and reasonable.

Wilmar was afraid. He knew how addictive cards could be, but he talked himself into going back, even though he wasn't gambling at the time. He called his old boss, who asked if he was ready to do it right. Wilmar's old sinful pride was certainly ready, so there they were twenty years later. He sold the bar, took almost all the proceeds from the sale, and went to Las Vegas. That night he drank alcohol, which affected his focus. Not surprisingly, he made mistakes, and in three days he lost fifty thousand dollars—money designated to support his family the following year.

This was yet another heartbreaking chapter in Wilmar's life. Most people might assume such a setback would drive a person to the brink of despair, but for Wilmar, it wasn't enough. Indeed, he wept bitterly, but he would gamble with his quitting. He would then give up one drug or abandon drinking. But this was a simple feat for him, as he would merely replace one vice with another. It would be like fasting ice cream while adding half-and-half to your coffee. He'd stop gambling but then do cocaine. It was a Sid Vicious cycle.

A Dream

A man named Job once said that God speaks one way, then another. Following a night at the bar, where he lost all his money, Wilmar had an inspiring dream during his drive home, sparking the concept for a new product range. The dream was so vivid that when he woke up, he wrote down every detail, including what the logo would look like.

He was furiously working away on the idea when one of his daughters came upstairs and asked him what he was doing. Wilmar excitedly told her about the dream and how he believed he could get a copyright and revolutionize the market. She got a glass of water, looked at her dad, told him how random that was, and went back to her room. In the weeks that followed, to the exclusion of everything else, Wilmar focused intensely on details, passionately fine-tuning everything. His fixation prompted the kids to ask their mom when Dad was going to get over it. She told them not to worry, that it was just a phase that would soon pass.

Wilmar still had some money from the bar sale, which he poured much of into product development, roping in his sons to help after school hours. But nothing was working, and that money was almost gone. And then he started using crack cocaine.

CRACK PARTY

With crack, you can start losing everything you care about. Chemistry was missing from Wilmar's marriage but not his body. His addictions were in full throttle and worsening. His wife and children were no longer his number one priority, and he was losing them. He tried to keep promises with his wife and the kids but broke them repeatedly. They'd make plans as a family, but he would come up with an excuse and cancel them—not because he wasn't physically able or didn't have time. He wanted to party with crack instead. Wilmar again ran the stop sign. He ignored the warning not to "go there."

Crack cocaine, sometimes called "rock" or "black rock" is incredibly destructive. It is far more potent and addictive than regular cocaine. Because the "high" users experience is so pleasurable—but very short—they need more of the drug to maintain it.

Crack snared Wilmar and initially hit all the highs. Wilmar could eat normally and go to bed when he wanted to. It was deceptively calming. The devil's lie. He thought it was just what he needed. But after a few uses, it ruled over his life, giving him insomnia, overpowering paranoia, and a horrific crash into depression.

Despite his crack addiction worsening, Wilmar was finally ready to produce and sell his new business product, but he needed to rent a kiosk to do so. His only viable option was to borrow against the $15,000 equity he had left in their house . . . . He started doing shows, but none of his pitches succeeded in orders. Wilmar was literally escorted outside in some places. Many weeks in, he had sold only eighty items and still had three hundred left. His family was stone broke, their financial situation pretty grim.

CATCHING A BREAK

But then Wilmar suddenly caught a break. A satisfied customer called to say Wilmar's product had changed his life. He invited Wilmar to have a spot at his home furnishing show. Wilmar readily agreed and took his remaining three hundred units of the product line to the show.

Wilmar by now needed to be high on cocaine to function. He was on the right highway. Just constantly in the wrong lane. To raise money to support his lifestyle, Wilmar sold stock in the start-up company to friends and family. But others kept trying to hijack his ideas and product line. He even had his own Judas. Friends deceived him and tried to start their own line of home goods, while big companies tried to manufacture similar products and undercut his income potential.

It's All Over

By spring 2007, the board did a hostile takeover. He and his wife were fired and the company was close to being sold. The power in his house was cut. His family was facing foreclosure and drowning in debt. For her, the party was over. She'd had enough and left for good.

Wilmar managed to get another home, but everything around him continued to disintegrate. Some may wonder if Wilmar had hit rock bottom. No. Not yet. Personal rock bottoms are moments when addicts are completely and genuinely surrendered. And Wilmar, incredibly, was still fighting. He needed one more chance—his life's theme song. Whether it was about money, traffic violations, his wife, or career, he always had a need for one more chance. The pattern had no end.

A Gift from God

For addicts, gambling isn't about winning. It's about betting. For thirty years or more, he kept betting. Play through, stay in the game until the trend changes. And for Wilmar, it did.

Wilmar's smartest move a year earlier had been applying for a patent. Three years later, the U.S. Government awarded Wilmar U.S. Patent 7461424. From that time on, he called his product line MyPillow.

The patent was a gift from God. Ruthless investors were now powerless to destroy him and take what he had built from the ground up. The company was securely in Wilmar's hands. He began dispatching salespeople out to shows with his product line. His business was soaring. So was his crack cocaine use.

Wilmar was like a cue ball. Instead of bumpers on a pool table, he bounced from one street dealer to another. Until there came a time when even his friends said enough is enough. Wilmar had been awake fourteen days straight. What was crazy was the friends were crack dealers. They had known him a long time and were genuinely concerned about him. That may sound strange. But Wilmar represented hope to them. Repeatedly he told them that one day he would be successful, that he would write a book. They'd scoffed at the idea, but inwardly they hoped he would succeed. His optimism and his business dream offered them hope to break their own addiction cycle and get clean themselves. His downward spiral represented a threat to their dream of being drug free and living a normal life. So, this unlikely group of good Samaritans orchestrated a plan. The word went out on the street: Nobody was to sell Wilmar any dope. No one.

Sure enough, he went out to score some crack. But everywhere he went, the answer was the same. Hours later he returned home, where a surprise party of three waited. His friends performed an intervention, forcing him to get sober, even staying with him to make him sleep.

Not long after the intervention, Wilmar was interviewed on a small public access station to talk about the business and his products. Most days the show aired at three in the morning, then Wilmar would get calls following his appearances. But one of the calls was very different. In his book *What Are the Odds? From Crack Addict to CEO*, Wilmar recalled being by himself at about ten o'clock at night, when a woman called. No. She wasn't calling to order. She explained that God had been telling her to call Wilmar and pray with him. She told him that what he was doing was important and not to ever give up. She prayed with him, then hung up. He believed the call was a sign from God.

Less than an hour later he got another call from a different lady. She explained that she had seen him on Channel 6 and had been praying for him. She kept hearing from the Lord in prayer that she was to call Wilmar and tell him that what he was doing was important. His product line was a platform for something far greater. Then they prayed for about thirty minutes. Two more complete strangers called with comparable messages. The experience caused him to wonder if God could have a larger plan for him. But he was so lost, the very thought of it made him feel terrible. Getting clean was not something he was eager to do. Public speaking wasn't particularly attractive either. So, he put the idea on the backburner and did nothing for an entire year.

That December he got an unexpected visit from his best friend. Wilmar used to buy drugs from him, and they "used" together as well. Wilmar had a high regard for him because he was the only one Wilmar knew who did drugs as often as he did. But Wilmar was surprised to learn his friend had been clean for several years. The conversation turned serious. Wilmar valued his friend's opinion—an addict who understood an addict's thought process. The exchange deeply affected Wilmar and got him thinking. Maybe he, too, could get clean and make a big comeback.

New Year's Day had come and gone several weeks before when one of Wilmar's sisters called. She told him that God had a platform for him. Moreover, the product line was a platform for something far greater. This conversation was not new. She asserted that God was tired of waiting and of Wilmar riding the fence. The door was going to shut, she warned, and someone else would be chosen. Her words hit home. He knew it was time and not one more day could go by. She prayed for his deliverance. Wilmar fell to his knees and asked God to wake him in the morning forever cleansed of all desire for tobacco, alcohol, cocaine, crack, or any other drug. Everything.

Physical Healing

The next day Wilmar woke up and felt something had changed, but he couldn't explain it. He felt like a different person. His brain fog was gone. Then a real eye opener—his insatiable hunger for crack and alcohol was gone! As weeks turned into months, other marvelous things started happening. There were more attempts to take his company, but they failed. Just a few months earlier he had been penniless, but now he was able to raise $30,000. Unbelievable!

Emotional Healing

He'd been clean for sixty days when a man invited him to a faith-based recovery group unlike any other support group Wilmar had gone to before. Those previous groups began with participants admitting their mistakes, acknowledging they hurt the ones they loved, and instituting a plan of reconciliation. But these programs always left Wilmar feeling awful about himself and he would quit.

This new group employed a different approach and led to discussions about his childhood, his father's abandonment, and childhood trauma. This treatment program resonated with Wilmar, whose parents divorced when he was in second grade. Working through the scars left by childhood trauma was a huge step. In the end, therapy and the various resources available played significant roles in Wilmar's journey towards sobriety and emotional healing.

Along the way, Wilmar discovered he had traits shared by not only addicts but entrepreneurs too. He had given all the credit for his work to his constant companion cocaine, yet he couldn't explain why he needed the junk to do his job. Through counseling, he learned how to sit in uncomfortable situations instead of trying to escape them. He could no longer pretend they didn't exist until one raised its head and he was forced to deal with it. Wilmar also learned how to avoid the pattern of negative thinking. He went from looking at his past as wasted time to realizing how much he had learned as an addict.

TODAY

Michael James "Wilmar" Lindell is a follower of Jesus Christ and a servant of the Lord today. His resourcefulness is a deterrent to addiction, but also a huge advantage in business. He runs a company with 1,600 or more employees, and he views everything the company does as less demanding and easier than his previous complicated, addiction-fueled life. He is no longer always hiding his addiction from people, and his double life is over.

His experiences equipped him with powerful tools for entrepreneurship. Some of his best workers are former addicts in need of a breakthrough, and he's willing to give it to them. He also founded the nonprofit Lindell Foundation that offers invaluable support to former addicts by aiding them in accessing treatment and various other services. This foundation also facilitates a recovery network, effectively connecting individuals battling addiction with others who have navigated the tumultuous journey of drug addiction and emerged successful in their recovery process. Lindell has even become friends with a former president of the United States.

Michael James Lindell's life is an incredible story of failure and redemption. He would say to anyone asking how to achieve his measure of success: Never stop trying, and follow God.

*Help with addictions is found at Lindell
Recovery Network. Contact them at*
lindellrecoverynetwork.org/

RESOURCES

Ashish Bhatt, MD, "Crack Cocaine and Abuse."
TheAddictionCenter.com, n.d..

ICTV, "'My Pillow' CEO Mike Lindell, on
Business, Drugs, Recovery & Trump." April 15,
2020, *ICTV.org.*

Joey Keogh, "Inside The MyPillow Guy's
Relationship With His Ex-Wife." *The List.Com,*
n.d., Updated: March 1, 2022.

Mike Lindell, *What Are the Odds? From Crack Addict
to CEO.* P. 214. Chaska, MN: Lindell Publishing,
LLC, 2019.

Patrizia Rizzo, SEO Reporter, "Keep It Lin the
Family: Who are Mike Lindell's children?" *The
US Sun,* April 21, 2021; updated Aug 12, 2021.

GOD AND ADDICTIONS

Being a Christian offers an addict multiple ways to break free, thanks to faith, prayer, and community.

Faith in God gives you hope and purpose, helping you overcome your struggles and helping you believe you are worth a healthier life. Christ's redemption, forgiveness, and ongoing transformation have turned millions of lives around on a new path of possibilities.

Prayer—both talking with God and listening to Him—fills you with comfort and strength, and His voice can reduce stress and anxiety, which are often triggers for substance use. Prayer and journaling can also serve as a form of reflection, helping you recognize and confront the issues contributing to your addiction.

Your Christian community can provide a strong support network. Churches often offer resources such as counseling services, support groups, or addiction recovery programs. Being part of a community can help combat feelings of isolation and provide encouragement and accountability during the recovery process.

Recovery is most effective when Christian programs are combined with professional medical treatment and therapy. Addiction is a complex issue that often requires a multifaceted approach.

8

TABLOID

One woman lay dead, a man lay wounded, and the gun was in his hand. As he looked around, stunned, the looks on the faces of multiple witnesses confirmed his worst fears. The woman would never spend time with her family again, would never hold her children, would never be hugged by her parents. Her life was snuffed out far too soon, and it was partly his fault.

***

Zander's parents, Carol and Rae, met at Syracuse University. In the early 1950s the family moved to Amityville, New York. Amityville, or "A-ville," as the locals prefer, includes the beach along the waterfront of Great South Bay with its spectacular view. Many notables have called Amityville home, including Buffalo Bill's Wild West Show markswoman, Annie Oakley, and the notorious gangster Al Capone. But then there's also the so-called ghost tour and paranormal sightseeing operations who refer to Amityville as a "zombie hamlet."

Rae taught social studies and coached football at Massapequa High School and Carol was a homemaker. In 1958, their eldest, whom they affectionately called "Zander," was born. Raising their large Irish Catholic family on a schoolteacher's salary in Suffolk County required some good math skills, but Carol knew the value of a dollar and how to make ends meet, so the family never lacked for anything. There was lots of fun around the dinner table and lively discussions about current events and community issues. Carol even thought her oldest son might someday occupy the White House.

Zander and his brothers were very competitive in Little League and football, something their father instilled in them. Around their Cape Cod house with fading green shutters, the boys teamed up with their Nassau Shores neighborhood buddies to play sports or put together one-act plays. The ragtag group made home movies using their father's camera, which he used to film rival football teams, but the boys made horror films with lots of ketchup. That was merely make-believe fun, but Zander would be just sixteen when a real horror took place on Ocean Avenue, just blocks from his home: the brutal murder of the DeFeo family, which led to the book and film The *Amityville Horror.* The brutal crime was somewhat of a prelude for Zander. In the distant future, he would face his own horror show.

There wasn't a lot of money for extras, so when they were old enough, the children went to work. Zander earned extra cash in between sports practices at Alfred G. Berner High School, doing odd jobs like bussing tables thirty-three miles away at Studio 54, Manhattan's famous discotheque.

A YOUNG ADULT

When he graduated from high school, Zander headed off to Washington, D.C., where he studied theater, eventually becoming a member of the Actors Studio. He landed his first Broadway role, only to have the production shut down three months later. But he'd gotten his foot in the door, and he went on to appear in eight other productions, earning a Tony Award nomination along the way. Zander next delved into television with roles in dramatic, musical, and comedy shows, garnering thirty-plus award nominations and critical acclaim.

Zander was generous, too, with his time, gifts, and support for various causes. As noteworthy as these activities and achievements were, it was his offstage behavior which made tabloid headlines.

LOVE AND MARRIAGE

In 1990, Ann and Zander were introduced at a script-reading session. A southern girl by birth, would turn out to be a bulldog in more than one regard. They began dating immediately and had what some described as a very intense, torrid relationship. The future *Getaway* costars married at Zander's Long Island Beach home surrounded by friends and family.

The couple brought wealth and fame to their marriage. But also tucked away in their Samsonites were some extras they should have left behind. He packed pride, arrogance, and an anger management problem, which was also noted when on set. And nicely folded in her bag was a history of panic attacks and agoraphobia.

Though raised Catholic, Zander had one of the worst tempers in the entertainment industry. For example, Zander's temper got the best of him when a photographer got too close to Ann and their three-day-old daughter outside their Los Angeles home.

AN UGLY DIVORCE

The objects of Zander's ire weren't always so deserving of it. The couple's daughter was five when the rocky, vitriolic, and very public divorce proceedings started. Zander's battle with Ann was bitter. It dragged on for years, costing the couple millions. His daughter was eleven when the divorce was finalized.

The Bible warns "Whatever you have said in the dark will be heard in the light, and what you have whispered in private rooms shall be proclaimed on the housetops" (Luke 12:3). Knowingly or unknowingly, Zander tested this biblical truth. In a moment of frustration, he thoughtlessly left a hurtful voicemail on his daughter's phone when she was twelve.

Somehow the private message got leaked to the entertainment news source TMZ.com, and the "tab mags" ran with it. Social media picked up the troubling story and spread it like wildfire in newspapers, television, and on the internet. Zander's visitation rights were temporarily suspended. Deeply embarrassed and ashamed, Zander regretted speaking to his daughter so hatefully. It took a while, but eventually he and his daughter reconciled, but not before a firestorm of public and private criticism rained down. All the nominations, accolades, and awards no longer mattered.

In later humility, Zander wrote in a memoir that if the goal of his ex and her lawyers was to ruin his relationship with his daughter, then he certainly gave them the ammunition to do that, and they succeeded. His relationship with his daughter was permanently harmed by that episode.

Then there was the incident when Zander was on board an American Airlines flight at LAX. He was playing a game on his phone while awaiting takeoff and became obstreperous when the flight attendant asked him to turn off his phone. Airport police removed him from the plane.

As if challenging the authority of a flight attendant while sitting in business class wasn't enough, Zander elected to ride first class with the police. One beautiful May morning he rode his bicycle against traffic, going the wrong way on 5th Avenue. The NYPD stopped him and he became belligerent. With no identification on his person, Zander got the choice bulkhead seat all to himself in the back of the patrol car. He was charged with the original traffic violation plus disorderly conduct, then released.

All alone, his mistakes were becoming too much to bear. Zander contemplated suicide. The split in his family had torn him apart, but he couldn't let himself wallow for long. Swallowing his pride, perhaps for the first time, Zander humbled himself and sought professional help. With counseling, he got back on track. The three-time Emmy award winner later reasoned if he *had* taken his life, Ann would have considered that a victory, and he wasn't going to let her win that battle.

FINDING LOVE AGAIN

Zander had moved on when he happened upon the health-conscious Hillary sampling some pure food and wine. It was love at first sight, and they married sixteen months later at St. Patrick's Old Cathedral in New York City.

The Tony Award nominated actor and his yoga instructor wife had seven children together. They had a strong marriage, attributing the strength of their union to spending time with each other as if they were still dating. They worked to keep their marriage and family environment from becoming just another venue, and considered themselves a good team.

Over time, Zander developed a relationship with Jesus. His favorite thing to do in the mornings, before anyone else in the house got up, was sit and listen for God's quiet voice. Zander found the time spent with God strengthened and helped him get focused for the day. But despite his faith, his anger continued.

HIS DOWNFALL—HIS SINFUL PRIDE

Zander behaved as if he was better than anyone else, and that he had a right to judge and mock whoever he pleased. His sinful pride soon led him to the worst days of his life.

Remember, "it is sin to know what you ought to do and then not do it" (James 4:17). Zander played many roles, including an investigator and characters in productions where police officers were part of the fictional story. He cowrote "Tabloid," an episode of the police drama television series *Law and Order: SVU*. So, he should have known how to act around those who actually enforce the law for a living. Zander's notorious run-ins with the real police no doubt contributed to his jaundiced view of the people in blue. He hadn't been shy about criticizing them, especially regarding police shootings.

In August 2014, eighteen-year-old Michael Brown and an accomplice committed a robbery. They were stopped just a few blocks away from the scene, and following a struggle, Brown was fatally shot by a Ferguson, Missouri, police officer.

That December, Zander promoted the idea of selling T-shirts with the phrase "My hands are up. Please don't shoot me." Without the benefit of facts, others joined him, judging the matter prematurely. It's been said that the measure we use to judge others will be the measure used to judge us. Zander was later to find this to be true.

A grand jury impaneled to hear the case cleared the officer of wrongdoing. But their findings were rejected by lawyers representing Brown's family, who demanded a federal government investigation. In response to intense public outcry, the U.S.

Department of Justice carried out a thorough criminal investigation. It involved numerous FBI special agents, state and local detectives, forensic scientists, and one hundred purported eyewitness interviews. The DOJ/FBI published the report of their findings in March 2015, concluding overwhelmingly that Officer Darren Wilson acted in self-defense.

There are more eyebrow-raising posts, but the one that wins is Zander's posts about when a Huntington Beach (CA) police officer was talking to a man outside a convenience store when a struggle ensued, resulting in the officer allegedly drawing his gun and killing the subject. When he learned about the shooting, Zander became prophetically engaged with the future when he sarcastically posted to his million followers on Twitter, musing on how it must feel to wrongfully kill someone.

Annie Oakley, you recall, was a frequent visitor to "A–ville." She offered this advice to those wanting to improve their marksmanship: "Aim at a high mark and you will hit it." Perhaps bored with taking potshots at police officers, Zander indeed aimed higher, firing away at former Vice President Dick Cheney by mocking the time Cheney accidentally shot a friend in the face while quail hunting. In a direct message exchange with an unidentified person, Zander mocked Cheney for doing so.

Zander spoke out frequently against gun rights advocates and the NRA, saying the Second Amendment is not a moral credit card that buys a person all the guns they want. But Zander went too far in 2017 when he tweeted: "If the NRA funneled illegal (money)... I say we shoot Wayne LaPierre [National Rifle Association CEO] 1,000 times with a BB gun" (*Twitter*, Jan 23, 2018).

His anger continued. A few weeks before Thanksgiving in 2018, Zander punched a man in the face, resulting in an ambulance ride and hospital stay for the victim, allegedly over a parking spot. Zander was arrested and charged with assault and harassment.

EVIL THINKING

Zander's outbursts were the result of a pattern of evil thinking. Jesus said,

> "Don't you understand yet?" Jesus asked. "Anything you eat passes through the stomach and then goes into the sewer. But the words you speak come from the heart—that's what defiles you. For from the heart come evil thoughts, murder, adultery, all sexual immorality, theft, lying, and slander." (Matthew 15:16–19)

God hears our vows or declarations, public or private. Zander's scurrilous statements about guns and the police reflect sinful pride. An outspoken supporter of gun control, he was also a spokesman for the anti-gun lobby, and for anti-NRA and anti-Pro-Second Amendment activists.

Zander was swimming in the judgment of others. The irony here is that Zander had appeared in many films and television shows where guns were part of his character's wardrobe and role, but his pride prevented him from appreciating their value. He would never repent of his stance and felt he could do whatever he wanted when he wanted.

A DEADLY DAY

Zander's sinful pride in his intelligence surfaced in his public statements about his personal encounters with police officers and other authority figures. His sinful pride of intellect was exposed in his commentary about police-involved shootings. Clearly, he allowed incomplete media accounts of officer-involved shootings and the courtship of anti-gun enthusiasts to lull him like Delilah, leading to a momentary false sense of security about firearm safety during film production. He allowed this form of kryptonite to impact his thinking, and it was costly.

When we goofed up as kids, we called a do-over. Much older kids on golf courses do the same. They just call them mulligans (free strokes) when their tee shot lands in Neverland. Hollywood can reshoot an imperfect scene multiple times until it's deemed a wrap. Actors can get up and walk around, have a glass of wine, smoke a cigarette in between takes; then lie back down and pretend to be mortally wounded or even dead. But that's not how it works with real-world violence. There are no do-overs in the real world when someone makes a split-second decision to use lethal force. Zander discovered this truth in 2021.

While filming a Western he was also the producer of, Zander discharged a single round from a Colt 45 handgun he thought was a prop. The shot instantly killed a cinematographer and wounded the director.

Suddenly, Zander found himself cast as the leading man in a movie produced by the State of New Mexico criminal justice system. In real time he was playing the part of himself: Alexander "Zander" Rae Baldwin III, known to moviegoers everywhere as Alec Baldwin. His question had been answered. Now he knew exactly how it felt to kill someone. Be careful what you wish for. You might just get it.

Sixteen months later, the Santa Fe, New Mexico, district attorney filed formal charges against Baldwin, the film's armorer, and an assistant film director over the shooting. Citing charging documents, writer

Chris McKee said Baldwin and the others originally faced the possibility of criminal charges for Hutchins' death. The assistant film director who allegedly handed Baldwin the gun that killed Hutchins was charged with the misdemeanor of negligent use of a deadly weapon and sentenced to six months unsupervised probation. Later, the charges against Baldwin and the others were dismissed pending further investigation.

Jesus proclaimed that every thoughtless or idle utterance can be used to judge the speaker. Even the minutest sin or the tiniest straying from God's perfection can result in a person being deemed guilty in the eyes of God.

> Don't speak evil against each other, dear brothers and sisters. If you criticize and judge each other, then you are criticizing and judging God's law. But your job is to obey the law, not to judge whether it applies to you. God alone, who gave the law, is the Judge. He alone has the power to save or to destroy. So what right do you have to judge your neighbor? (James 4:11–12)

According to English actor and social critic Os Guinness, a good rule to practice before judging others is to recognize that all the known facts are not all the facts, and a second rule to practice before judging others is to understand things are not always as they seem. He says that the smart move is to wait until the fire is put out before diagnosing how it started. That way you don't get burned.

In spite of his faith, Alec Baldwin never heeded the Bible's teaching about judgment.

FORGIVENESS

Despite Baldwin's pride, the important lesson is that God would rather forgive than judge. God ultimately viewed him as a man of faith in His final assessment. This is substantiated by Samson's inclusion in the biblical "Hall of Fame." As we peruse the roster of names inscribed there, it becomes clear that none of the individuals in this "hall of faith" were without flaws, just like Baldwin. Thank goodness. He is ready to encounter us exactly in our current state and guide us to where He desires, if only we permit Him.

The important thing is not where Alec Baldwin has been. It's where he's going.

RESOURCES

Benjamin VanHoose, "Alec Baldwin Finds 'Inner Peace' in Morning When It's 'Totally Silent: I Spend That Time with God.'" *People Magazine,* January 19, 2022.

"Department of Justice Report Regarding The Criminal Investigation into the Shooting Death of Michael Brown by Ferguson, Missouri Police Officer Darren Wilson." *Justice.gov,* March 4, 2015: justice.gov/sites/default/files/opa/press releases/attachments/2015/03/04/doj_report_on _shooting_of_michael_brown_1.pdf.

Elle Collins, "Alec Baldwin's Complicated History In Hollywood": www.looper.com/650028/the-untold-truth-of-alec-baldwin. Updated February 10, 2023.

Jake Epstein, "Alec Baldwin has a history of opposing the NRA and gun rights activists." *Insider,* Oct. 22, 2021.

Nicole Chenoweth, Katherine Schaffstall, and M. L. Nestel, "'How It Must Feel': Alec Baldwin tweet about 'wrongfully killing someone' resurfaces as star shoots crew member dead in horror accident." *The US Sun,* n.d., Updated: September 2022.

God's Forgiveness

God, through the death and resurrection of Jesus Christ, has forgiven the sins of those who accept Him as their Lord and Savior. This divine act of forgiveness serves as a model for Christians to emulate in their own lives.

In the New Testament of the Bible, particularly in the Gospels, Jesus speaks frequently about the importance of forgiveness. Jesus said, ""If you forgive those who sin against you, your heavenly Father will forgive you. But if you refuse to forgive others, your Father will not forgive your sins" (Matthew 6:14–15). This passage emphasizes the reciprocal nature of forgiveness in Christianity—just as God forgives us, we are expected to forgive others.

Christian forgiveness involves letting go of resentment, anger, and desire for revenge against those who have wronged us. It doesn't mean forgetting the offense or denying the pain caused. Instead, it's choosing to release the burden of the past and move forward. This act of forgiveness can lead to healing, reconciliation, and peace.

However, it's important to note that forgiveness in Christianity doesn't equate to condoning harmful actions or allowing oneself to be repeatedly harmed. It's about liberating oneself from the bitterness and resentment that can hinder spiritual growth.

Ultimately, Christian forgiveness reflects the grace and mercy of God. It's a powerful act of love and a testament to the transformative power of the Christian faith.

9

DISCIPLINED

Weaving, they circled each other. Lunging and grappling, neither finding a sure hold. Minutes ticked on like hours. Daniel was getting tired. He could feel the exhaustion dragging on his steps, slowing his movement. *I have to keep going*, he told himself. *Breathe, watch for your opening. There! I have him!* His arms and legs found position and his opponent was pinned. Daniel had won. He let go and got shakily to his feet. The cheers sounded distorted as exhaustion and excitement swept over him. Overwhelmed by a myriad of emotions, he began to weep.

***

Every village has a lynchpin that holds various elements of the community together before the wheels fall off. For St. Paris, Daniel is one such person, a native son whose grandfather and great-grandfather worked the land. They were lynchpins too. One farmer helped another keep it together. But Daniel would not follow them. He toils in another field.

Daniel grew up on the outskirts of Urbana, Champaign County, in a two-parent household. Daniel's mother Shirley ran a housecleaning business. John, Daniel's dad, was old school. He worked all day—putting new cars together and then coaching Little League, teaching young ballplayers to work together. Daniel, his brother Jeff, and all their buddies were a little afraid of John. He had a presence that encouraged their toeing the line around him. They all wanted him to be their coach, and they would give 100 percent for him not only on the baseball field, but on the wrestling mat too.

Daniel was in third grade when he first became interested in organized amateur wrestling, thanks in part to John loving the sport. Daniel and Jeff became the core of the kids' wrestling program at Graham Elementary. "Let 'em wrestle" John would plead to officials during matches. That's the kind of father figure he was. He had a huge impact on not just Daniel and his younger brother, but also their extended family, cousins, and everyone they wrestled with in Champaign County, as well as their non-wrestling friends. His dad invested quite a bit of himself into Daniel's wrestling, even setting up a practice gym for him in the family garage.

Daniel was only nine years old when he won his first national championship. When he entered Graham High, he joined its wrestling team, the Falcons, where his coach set the groundwork for character traits that would define Daniel's approach to life. At every practice, his coach emphasized self-discipline as the most important quality for accomplishing one's goals.

Daniel was an unyielding competitor, claiming four state high school wrestling titles (with his record of 150-1 still unbroken), and two NCAA wrestling championships—where he triumphed over a future Olympic medalist. Graham's wrestling squads clinched fourteen straight state championships and two national titles. His high school academic and athletic achievements were outstanding. But Daniel was just warming up.

Daniel's home was also notable among high school wrestlers. If you were to walk in the doors of Daniel's home in those days, you would not see trophies, plaques, or celebratory banners. What you would find in the converted garage was a full-size wrestling mat. Daniel's "gym" became well-known as a "practice field" for many of the region's wrestlers. They got to "practice" one way or another, carrying their water bottles, headgear, and obligatory sport bag and full of smack talk. but in the end, they were all friends. Though their tank tops were different colors and bore different school names, as brothers in sport, they were all on the same side. But once they stepped on the regulated mat, they were fierce opponents. Ironically, Daniel was decisioned in match number 127, losing at the hands of a fellow grappler and friend from Watkins Memorial High who had trained in Daniel's own gym.

LOVE CAME EASILY

Daniel had been one of the most exceptional wrestlers to ever don the singlet for the Graham Falcons. But he knew nothing about fishing. Therefore, no one was surprised when he got hooked by Anne, an honors student at Graham High. Their courtship began when he was thirteen and she fourteen. She and Daniel were actually introduced by her brothers, who were also wrestlers. They were great guys, but she was one of a kind. An athlete in her own right, Anne was a member of the Graham Falcon's thinclad's 2 mile and 1 mile relay team that set the girl's school record at 4:09:9. Anne also competed in the 100-meter low hurdles.

Daniel also ran cross-country, no doubt to keep up with Anne. She ran circles around him and he loved it. A year ahead of Daniel, Anne was practically the girl next door—her home was less than a mile from Daniel's. They dated throughout high school. Anne graduated with honors, earning a scholarship honor award.

He had blazed his way through high school. Now he was ready for the next level. Following his freshman state championship win, Coach McCunn always thought Daniel had a shot. McCunn knew he *could* do it. He just didn't know if he *would* do it. The difference between a good wrestler and a state champion level wrestler is their mental attitude. But Daniel never lost his mental toughness. He had good mat sense. He knew he could. On a crisp Wednesday morning, with family and friends in attendance, Daniel signed a national letter of intent, committing himself to wrestle for the University of Wisconsin Badgers.

COLLEGE

The first of his family to go to college, Daniel pursued a bachelor's degree in economics from the University of Wisconsin, and also joined the wrestling team there. Anne also went to Wisconsin, where their courtship continued. He wrestled for the Division 1 Badgers, pinning opponents and winning by decision. She got pinned when Daniel asked for her hand in marriage.

Daniel found the grind of collegiate wrestling far more physical and intense than anticipated. Collegiate wrestling has its unique characteristics. Predominantly an American sport, it places emphasis on the duration a competitor maintains control on the mat, as opposed to the lifts and throws preferred in international competitions. It values dominance and control over risk and explosiveness.

Champion wrestlers are challenged month after month, to maintain their weight in their respective weight classes. The ups and downs of the wrestling season, weight management, bumps and bruises, wins and losses, and nagging injuries are all part of the "grind" of a wrestling season. And they must keep their grades up too. Everyone is pretty evenly matched, so victory would hang in the balance by Daniel's mental approach to each match. One rule he learned quickly was a wrestler can never afford to lose concentration. A momentary distraction and you could find yourself thrown home for the holidays.

Some wrestling contests are best described as tactical matches, with each wrestler waiting for an opening. A wrestler might achieve that towards the end of a period, executing a surprise takedown at the mat's edge, seemingly catching his opponent off guard to score points. However, the tables can turn just as swiftly when he suffers a similar lapse of focus, and now the difference is merely one escape point. Wrestling is an intense, close-combat sport, where rankings play a minimal role during the seven-minute bout within the circle. A single mistake, a missed move, or a poorly timed action can result in the referee's hand striking the mat, signifying the end of a match.

Daniel had to work harder, still determined to succeed. His high school coach's training in self-discipline would serve him well. He says all fall short in being self-disciplined, but working to be self-disciplined is a lesson he learned from Coach McCunn, who impacted many people in addition to wrestlers. He discovered that victory often requires battling for what matters. Too frequently, individuals are ready to concede even before the referee initiates the game with a whistle blow. However, it's not solely about the struggle; it's equally about the cause behind the fight. He would make this his legacy.

Even with all his work, he almost lost the state championship, trailing in the second period. It's been said in wrestling that you're going to feel pressure or expectations—from fans, family, coaches, teammates, or yourself. Pressure will find you. The pressure in the title match had been intense. Still, he managed to pull off the win. With the state championship victory in hand, Daniel wept. When he stepped onto the podium that evening, the mob of Graham High fans gave him a one-minute standing ovation. The Badger standout was voted most dedicated athlete on his team for three consecutive seasons.

Unlike every other story in this book, Daniel was not filled with sinful pride. He listened to his elders and implemented their wisdom. He kept obeying the Lord, and he never thought more of himself than the Lord allowed. He put God first in everything. This is a story of godly humility, and the success and influence one man can have for the good when he listens, trusts, and obeys the Lord.

Marriage

Anne and Daniel returned home, where she became an art teacher in Champaign County. Up to that point, Anne had worn his varsity "G" letter jacket. Soon she would wear his ring. When they married, Daniel had truly entered the Winner's Circle. The newlyweds returned to Madison, where they shared a one-bedroom apartment near the hospital and Wisconsin campus.

Eventually Daniel and Anne elected to put down roots on Kanagy Road, close to where they'd grown up. They settled in among familiar, rambling country roads, bordered by miles of cornfields; and just as they had been mentored and encouraged, so they eagerly gave back. Anne initially homeschooled their children. When she wasn't working with her own children, Anne was an assistant junior high track coach, but she later became a public schoolteacher.

Early in their marriage, Daniel was well on his way to securing a head coach position. However, the birth of their last child ignited a spark in him to delve into politics. Craving a fresh challenge and driven by the desire to effect change for families, he stepped into this new arena. As his own family grew, he became increasingly cognizant of the significance of family. As conservatives, they lived a life of faith, family, and community.

MASTERING HIS FUTURE

After his time at UW, Daniel went on to earn a master's in education and a law degree, all while raising a growing family. His focus shifted from wrestling to public service in 1994, when he secured a seat in the Statehouse that became available due to a retirement. Despite being a novice in politics, he triumphed over a county commissioner in the GOP primary. This victory was essentially equivalent to winning the election in the conservative region of the state. Believing wholeheartedly that family is the backbone of America, he wanted to represent the moms, dads, and families he would have the privilege of representing.

Daniel ran many miles cross-country, but the Defender of Life Award winner drove even more miles in public service across the state, even holding the position of chairman for the Republican Study

Committee, the most substantial caucus in the House of Representatives. Yet, he always managed to attend to his family's needs. In 2006, Daniel made a bold move to campaign for Congress and effortlessly secured his victory for the 4th Congressional District seat in the state. Supporters say he has represented his constituents well, winning multiple reelection victories.

COMPARING WRESTLING TO POLITICS

Daniel considers the wrestling mat an ideal foundation for life's battles, including politics. Committee hearings are the closest thing to wrestling matches, he notes. He considers his years in St. Paris and around Champaign County—growing up on the mat, learning the sport and raising a family—as determinative to a prominent career in Washington, D.C.

Wrestlers start off a match in the "neutral" position—meaning both grapplers are on their feet and facing each other. But there's no neutrality for Daniel regarding the subjects he's passionate about. As a staunch defender of American values, Daniel's feet are firmly planted on God-honoring principles, such as fighting to defund Planned Parenthood and protecting same-sex sports, freedom of speech, and the right to speak out against the government. Nothing is more basic, Daniel insists. To never get to the truth would bring discredit to his job as a public servant.

He asserts that an excessive number of individuals are conforming to the "woke" movement, rather than taking a stand and expressing gratitude for the nation that provided them with opportunities to achieve their goals. There are unintended consequences when students are taught to hate their country, or that their country is not great. Daniel loves his country and represents the pillars of American success and greatness, and he is a steadfast believer that conservatism is rooted in four fundamental principles: robust defense, tax reduction, decreased spending, and the protection of Christianity and traditional American values.

FURTHER ACCOMPLISHMENTS OF DANIEL

In 2007, Daniel earned a position on the House Oversight Committee. He played a significant role in exposing a covert gun trafficking operation known as "Fast and Furious," which supplied AK-47s to Mexican drug syndicates. Daniel also spotlighted millions of dollars of unnecessary expenditure in the previous administration's multiple Green Energy Programs and opposed the Justice Department's "Operation Choke Point" program aimed at law-abiding firearm owners.

In 2015, Daniel, along with eight other conservative Republicans, established the House Freedom Caucus. He clarified that the reason for creating the caucus was to represent numerous Americans who felt disregarded by Washington. Their objective is to advocate for transparent, accountable, and limited government, adherence to the Constitution and the rule of law, and policies that foster freedom, safety, and prosperity for all Americans.

Daniel spearheaded the exposure of one of the most significant scandals in the history of the Treasury Department. His investigation led the Treasury Department Inspector General and the Oversight Committee to discover that the IRS was deliberately targeting conservative groups.

In 2016, Daniel collaborated with then-Representative Mike Pompeo to probe and publish a report on the lethal attack on our embassy in Benghazi, Libya. His efforts also revealed misconduct at the highest echelons of the United States Government, challenging senior Justice Department officials for obstructing Congress and their allegations of Russian interference in the election. In 2023, Daniel was appointed the ranking member of the House Judiciary Committee.

A pinnacle moment in Daniel's career was when he received the Presidential Medal of Freedom from President Donald J. Trump. This esteemed award is the highest civilian honor in the nation, bestowed by the president upon individuals who have made exceptional contributions to the security or national interests of the United States, to global peace, or to cultural and other important ventures.

Daniel remains a beacon of inspiration to all Americans who cherish freedom, and he has established himself as one of the most influential members of his generation in Congress.

INFLUENCE AND SUCCESS

Daniel never seemed to realize the influence he had on other grapplers. According to the Fellowship of Christian Athletes, a sports campus ministry, there are three types of competitors: some are either very talented but not hardworking or not very talented but very hardworking, or there's the rare competitor who recognizes their God-given talent and works diligently to develop it for the glory of the Lord. Daniel never forgot the source of his skill, and his performance has inspired many younger kids to follow their own athletic passions. They saw his back-to-back titles and believed they could win too. He was far more inspiring to other wrestlers than a dust-gathering trophy.

Three decades after leaving Graham High, the wrestling standout was inducted into the National Wrestling Hall of Fame, which highlights the wrestling community's admiration for those who have leveraged the sport's disciplines to embark on distinguished careers in various other fields. Daniel earned this honor for not only his wrestling but also his public service as an elected official. He also deserved it for his efforts in saving Olympic wrestling, being one of many voices instrumental in the International Olympic Committee (IOC) overturning the decision to remove freestyle and Greco-Roman wrestling from the 2020 Summer Games.

Likewise, his family's success doesn't fit on the mantle. It comes from years of dedication, knowledge, and talent. Each family member knew what they were doing on the mat of life and had outstanding execution. They learned to recognize an opponent's weakness and worked to defeat it. Preparation was their key then and remains so today.

Daniel knows he's blessed to have Anne and their children. Four decades after walking down the aisle, the happy two are going strong, helping their family and others step into the winner's circle. He's still a devoted follower of Badger football, and three of his four children attended UW and played sports. There was a time when his desk held a calendar meticulously marked with his children's athletic events, which he diligently made efforts to attend. He even served as a caddy for his daughter at golf tournaments. Nowadays, the calendar is filled with dates of his grandchildren's birthdays and their various activities.

For James Daniel Jordan and wife Polly Anne, there is no better place to be than to be in the will of the Lord. One day, they'll clean out his Capitol Hill office and say goodbye to the world of politics. Then Jim Jordan, Republican Member of Congress from Ohio, might be heard saying to Polly, "Wanna wrestle?"

RESOURCES

David Bilmes, Citizen Sports Editor, "State Champ Jordan Packs A Lot of Power." *The Urbana Daily Citizen*, March 14, 1979, P. 6, Retrieved June 13, 2023.

Karalee Geis, Capitol Hill Outreach Director, "Doing What We Said: An Interview with Congressman Jim Jordan." *Libertas* (Issue 42.1— Spring 2021) by Young America's Foundation, *Issuu.com*.

Lee Gordon, "Wrestling: a family affair for UW's Jordan," *The Badger Herald*, March 6, 2014.

Richard Immel, USA Wrestling, "Wrestling: A Family Affair for Ohio State All-American Bo Jordan." *TeamUSA.Org*, November 19, 2015.

Sabrina Eaton, "U.S. Rep. Jim Jordan of Ohio gains power among House conservatives," *Cleveland.com*, June 5, 2011.

Star Parker, "Who Is Jim Jordan?" *Creators.com*, April 25, 2018.

LIVING RIGHTEOUSLY

Because one person disobeyed God, many became sinners. But because one other person obeyed God, many will be made righteous.

God's law was given so that all people could see how sinful they were. But as people sinned more and more, God's wonderful grace became more abundant. So just as sin ruled over all people and brought them to death, now God's wonderful grace rules instead, giving us right standing with God and resulting in eternal life through Jesus Christ our Lord.

—Romans 5:19–21

Righteousness or living righteously involves:

Faith in Jesus Christ and acceptance of His sacrifice for humanity's sins. As stated in Romans 3:22, "We are made right with God by placing our faith in Jesus Christ. And this is true for everyone who believes, no matter who we are."

Growing in the fruit of the Spirit— love, joy, peace, patience, kindness, goodness, faithfulness, gentleness, and self-control (Galatians 5:22–23), so you can be like Jesus to those around you and reflect His love and grace.

Following God's moral and ethical standards outlined in the Bible. This includes honesty, integrity, and justice (Psalm 51:6; 106:3; John 1:47). Your actions should align with your faith, and you should always make choices that honor God.

Serving others. Following the example of Jesus, you are called to help those in need (Matthew 25:45), advocate for justice, and love your neighbors as yourself (Matthew 22:36–40) because every human is created by God and has infinite value.

Living righteously doesn't mean living perfectly. Everyone falls short and makes mistakes. However, through faith in Jesus Christ, repentance, and God's grace, you are forgiven if you fall and empowered to continue striving for righteousness.

Righteousness is about having a personal relationship with God, striving to emulate the character of Jesus, and living out your faith through action.

10

ENCOUNTER

Some details remain a little fuzzy. A deer appeared suddenly. Mo swerved around it. But she started losing control, the Jeep Cherokee fishtailing off the road into the median strip. Mo fought with the steering wheel, but it was a losing battle. The Jeep shot across the other side of the highway, hit an embankment, and rolled three times.

No one knows how long she was unconscious. When she came to, she was hanging upside down and choking. Mo lay in a ravine in what was left of the Jeep, completely alone, vomiting blood, and gasping for air. Her fame meant nothing anymore, and she didn't even know if she'd lose her life in the hours that followed.

***

Mo stood tall above most girls and many boys her age, even in elementary school, having inherited some of her beloved dad—"Big John's"—height. Big

John had played four seasons at Carson–Newman and passed his love of football on to Mo, and she could often be found at recess playing football with the boys. Her elementary school's recreation department had no football program for girls, and the boys' teams had full rosters. However, there was that other kind of football, the kind played in Brazil. In Cobb County, Georgia, they call it soccer.

At the age of seven, Mo started playing with a young girls' soccer team, and from 2002 to 2007, she had the honor of being part of the Georgia State ODP Team, playing a significant role in securing the Georgia State Cup title for her team in 2003. In the 2004 season, the team further distinguished itself by clinching the Disney Champions title, Raleigh Cup, and the prestigious Manchester United Cup National Championship.

Once Mo moved to Lassiter High School and played for the Lassiter Trojans, she was unstoppable, as her dad knew she would be. Big John was a big fan of the Lassiter Trojans, and he was known to strategically beat the rush to the snack bar at halftime, then hurry back so he wouldn't miss any of a game she was in. He was extremely proud of his daughter and always talked soccer with her at home.

SHOOK

Mo was quickly becoming one for coaches to watch—for her superb athletic ability, especially at goalie, where she excelled at an extremely high level. The school had great expectations of her. Mo stood tall, but when it came to having friends, she came up short, always on the outside looking in. At 6', 0" she was too tall to fit in. It mattered little what Mo could do on the soccer field, nor did it matter that she'd been in TV commercials and competed in pageants. Her soccer world popularity wasn't shared by classmates and did little to alleviate the games mean girls play. Just a fourteen-year-old girl, she couldn't control who accepted her, and the lack of it shook her.

Mo couldn't control her classmates' verbal abuse, nor her height, but her flesh was still hers to manage. That she could control. She journaled, meticulously recording what she ate, while fastidiously tracking calories. Mo confessed that she never specifically decided to stop eating, but that eating was one thing she could control, and it became all she focused on. She had done modeling and competed for the title of "Miss Georgia Teen" in pageants. Now the contest was for the title of "Miss Self-Concept."

John grew frustrated with his youngest daughter because eating meals had always been one of their special times together and she wouldn't eat. Instead of fellowship, their meals became adversarial, where only portions of hostility were served. Until one day when her digestive system said it had starved enough, and she convinced herself she should eat all the food she could find. Looking over the remnant of the battle just lost, Mo was convinced she'd gained ten pounds. Anxious and guilt-ridden, she was sure she'd instantly be "fat" and unacceptable—familiar thoughts that continued to make her hate herself. But anorexia was less about making her body thin than giving herself a measure of control and taking pride in her strong will. With this one episode of binge eating, the father of all lies mocked her, telling her she couldn't do it, that she was too weak to control it and never would.

"We are products of how we think." (Chip Ingram, Former West Liberty State College basketball player and evangelist)

HATING TO LOSE

Mo was so competitive that even in her cycle of self-destruction, she hated to lose. She rose to the liar's challenge, took the bait of sinful pride that she could control her eating, and rushed to the bathroom to "prove" that she was still in control and could "fix" this. Kneeling at the porcelain throne, she regurgitated it all. Not content with this one incident, Mo quickly started to bring up every meal.

She became proficient, purging nine or ten times daily. Like reacting to a penalty kick, purging became a trained response.

Mo had all the classic signs of bulimia, but sometimes the obvious isn't so obvious. No one said anything. Maybe that was because she was good at keeping secrets. Her secret life became a friend named "Mia Bull" (bulimia in reverse) she could count on.

Incredibly, Mo's performance on and off the soccer field continued to improve. Excelling in both high school and club competitions, she was invited to join the Georgia Olympic Development (ODP) team and fielded scholarship offers from several colleges. Alongside her sporting achievements, she also continued to pursue acting, modeling, and pageant competitions, where she found congeniality in the queen's court. She was a winner who took pride in her own brokenness, convincing herself that in spite of her hurt, brokenness, and emptiness, she had everything she had always wanted.

As time passed, she dropped her guard. She found herself unable to delay the urge to vomit. She couldn't provide the dentist with a reason for the erosion of her teeth, nor could she admit that frequent vomiting had worn away the enamel.

Unlike many, Mo never experienced a defining moment when she decided to put an end to her bulimia. She was convinced it was an unending battle, much like the one fought by one in every hundred teenage girls suffering from an eating disorder.

DESPERATE TO LEAVE

As one of the leading goalkeeper recruits in the 2008 class, Mo was honored as a Soccer Buzz Top 75 Recruit and ranked among the top six goalkeeper recruits in the US. Her impressive career record at Lassiter stood at 40-9-1, with 30 shutouts and only 28 goals conceded over three years. She concluded her high school career with an outstanding 0.42 average goals against and a save percentage of 0.94—all of which set new school records. At this point, Mo had secured a scholarship to play soccer at LSU and was eager to move beyond her time at Lassiter, and the title of Miss Self-Concept along with it.

"Resist the devil and he will flee from you."
(James 4:7)

In her senior year, Mo found herself sitting in her room praying. She had grown up in a culture of Christianity. Her family went to church on Sunday and Wednesday nights, and she attended FCA Friday mornings at school. If the family went to a wedding on a Saturday, that was a bonus. But Mo's faith journey was largely superficial and performance based, and in her pride, she had only trusted herself rather than Jesus. Now, however, she had to admit that she had no control at all. Her life had taken a disastrous turn. She was broken.

In the privacy of her room, Mo confessed to the Lord that she couldn't continue with the charade any longer. Then, at that precise moment, her mother, Heidi, walked in, carrying a basket of laundry. Heidi had no idea that the load she would leave with would be far heavier.

Pride Crashes to the Ground

The mindset of a goalie is to manage game-time emotions and see the game as a challenge rather than fear failure. On the field and in goal, Mo was a force to be reckoned with. Now the force that controlled her life was about to be reckoned with. The daughter who had hidden behind the pride of sports recognition was seriously ill. Her confession spewed out like projectile vomiting. Her hidden, secret life of bulimia, purging ten times a day and downing energy pills, roared out. The "I've got it all together" mask, worn for years and fooling everyone, instantly was torn away, revealing an All-American goalie with 235 game-winning saves desperately in need of the "save" of her own life. God's divine intervention would be her gamechanger.

Life took a transformative turn when Mo acknowledged her struggles. She sought help from a nutritionist and found solace in a support group dedicated to aiding those recovering from bulimia. The deceit ceased, and she began mending her strained relationship with her father. In the subsequent months, there were occasional setbacks, but she persisted, despite missing her friend "Mia Bull". Whenever that voice crept back, trying to pull her back to the lie that controlling her eating was a great idea, she prayed.

The National Eating Disorders Association (NEDA offers free individual and family support as well as awareness information on its website, https://www.nationaleatingdisorders.org. Or, email, info@NationalEatingDisorders.org.

On the field she was starting goalkeeper, recording shutouts in scrimmages against UNC and Duke. During the second half of one home match against Brigham Young, a foul was declared just beyond the perimeter of the goalkeeper's box. A teammate started to take the free kick, but Mo waved her off. Mo had been recruited, not just for her defensive play in goal, but also for her leg strength.

She stepped back, struck the ball, and thought, *Whoa* as it sailed over the awaiting players and landed just in front of the goalkeeper's box. The opposing keeper rushed forward but misjudged the ball's trajectory, then leaped as it bounced over her head and into the net!

The jubilant screams conveyed all Mo needed to know. In no time, she was encircled by a crowd of cheering and jumping young players. She joined in the dance and embraced her teammates, then lifted her gaze to the audience stands. There, beneath the press box, stood her father, his exuberant voice resonating above the rest. Mo later recalled seeing his smile stretch so wide that it seemed as though his teeth touched his ears for a good five minutes.

LSU won 4–1, and her dad managed to get the incredible play from ESPN! The athletic department furnished the tape, and twelve hours later they were fixated on *Sports Center's Top Ten Plays of the Week*, watching her incredible ninety-yard kick bounce into the opposing goal over and over again.

A New Way of Living

Away from the field, Mo became a keeper of the sheep. She spoke openly and passionately about topics others might consider off-limits, confessing a struggle with pornography from age nine to nineteen. About those years, Mo said she kept searching for a pleasure she couldn't find but that her mess of a testimony was redeemed by a King who makes our hopeless things holy.

Thriving throughout her freshman year, Mo became a transparent voice for truth. In His power, grace, and mercy, God scored a victory through Mo's authenticity. She knew God was not a keeper of wrongs and that He had removed her sins as far from her as the east is from the west (Psalm 103:12). His unfailing love and mercy helped her heal (v. 8).

BACK HOME

Compared to her previous four years, college life was confusing, but in the end found it very rewarding. But life wasn't the same back home. Mo's father called her ten times a day, texting her if she didn't answer. She knew he missed her. But just as her family had failed to recognize the signs of her eating disorder, Mo failed to recognize the signs of her father's depression.

At home on Christmas break, Mo and the family celebrated the New Year by attending the Chick-fil-A Bowl in Atlanta, when LSU pummeled Georgia Tech 38–3. Two days later, neither she, her mom, nor her sister Sloan had heard from their dad, who never failed to call home. It was odd, but with each passing hour, their anxiety grew until Heidi checked her emails and began screaming. He'd left a suicide note.

Heidi quickly called the suicide prevention hotline, who in turn summoned the police. Heidi and the girls then drove as fast as they could to his building. Cobb County Police were already there and had cordoned it off, but John's car was missing.

John left work that January afternoon, then wrote "the note." With his laptop and guns in hand, he left home for the last time. He drove 160 miles to Huntsville, Alabama, where he checked into the Hilton and shot himself in the chest. Sadly, John had used a permanent solution to solve a temporary problem.

The National Suicide and Crisis Lifeline three-digit number is 9–8–8. Alternatively, TEXT "Please Help" to 988 Suicide & Crisis Lifeline.

Mo deliberated taking the semester off but realized being back at LSU was where she needed to be. However, she tried hanging out with the same friends she'd partied with, the only people she really knew, but she was very quickly convicted by the Holy Spirit. Jesus called her away to a season of isolation with Him. She needed healing, restoration, and, ultimately, strength to say no to things that weren't good for her. It was in that season of saying yes to Jesus that He began sending the right kind of relationships, the right kind of friendships, the right community that she was seeking. The FCA lined the back wall at the funeral. They adopted her, becoming her campus family.

PRESSING ON

Miss Self-Concept had been guiding her emotions before. Now those days were over. Others were stepping up to help—the "FCA" people who had planted seeds of faith in high school and pressed in when she was hurting early in college Their leaders. Their coaches. The athletes who had surrendered their lives to Christ came to her rescue now—the same ones she had so blindly stiff-armed away. Suddenly, like Saul on the road to Damascus, she could see them rightly and how the seeds this sports ministry planted earlier had taken root and were growing in her.

The grief response is a physical, chemical, and emotional one. Mo developed dry skin, her hair fell out, and rashes appeared. There were new battles to fight—heavy colds, then strep. She cherished being away from noise. Over and over she watched a silent movie that she alone had a ticket to. She wondered what had gone through her dad's mind in the last dozen or so hours of his life. She pictured the hotel room and him, in despair, holding the gun. She lost herself in dark thoughts.

Seasons change and so did Mo. Her grades were as good as her game. Top shelf. She got invited to train with the U–23 national team. All her life, Mo had taken the escape route from situations that could have taken her further than she wanted to go. Now, her soccer and academic life were filling a void. In 2010, Mo was the proud recipient of the Wilma Rudolph Student Athlete Achievement Award. This prestigious award is given out yearly to student athletes who have triumphed over significant personal, academic, and emotional challenges to attain academic success while participating in intercollegiate sports. Wilma Rudolph was a world-class athlete. And so was Mo. But the direction of travel was different. The former sprinted toward gold. The latter sprinted *from* God.

WHY GOD?

Mo couldn't make sense of why her number one cheerleader was gone. Why did he bail out on them? She felt cheated. Expressing her thoughts aloud, she accused God of not caring because he allowed it to happen, saying that if He was truly all-knowing, he could have stopped her father. It was late 2010 and she was driving home for Thanksgiving and incredibly angry. Then she told God He was full of crap and fake, and that His love for her was not real either, challenging Him to show her He loved her, to show her in a way that she would know or He might as well just wreck her and end her life too. We've already learned God hears everything. And He certainly heard Mo.

Mo doesn't remember much of the accident itself, but in between moments of awareness, Mo felt peace. God's peace. The kind that surpasses all understanding. She knew. She knew there had been an encounter with God. It was the most intimate and incredible encounter she had ever known.

She was jolted awake by a sudden flash of light across her face, only to lose consciousness again almost instantly. The next thing she knew, she was in a hospital, being wheeled through a corridor on a bed. She remembers the murmur of voices. One of them was a retired Navy paramedic. "How could anyone survive this?" she heard him say. At first glance, she appeared only to have superficial cuts to her face and jaw. But he knew there was more. Bleeding from the ears testified she had a concussion. Nausea, vomiting, shortness of breath. Lung damage. Hours later an MRI would reveal a cracked vertebra, broken ribs, and a damaged liver.

OKAY ALREADY?

Sometimes God will stop us to get our attention. There was debate over Thanksgiving break about Mo's return to school. But she convinced everyone, including herself, that she could return. A friend drove her to Baton Rouge, but things quickly turned south. Mo passed out in the middle of her first class. Worse, she regained consciousness only to vomit on her desk. In beauty pageants they call that "blowin' the contest." It wasn't pretty. She withdrew from her classes and flew home. The next month and a half were spent in bed.

The more Mo replayed the accident, the more she saw God's hand in it. Of all the people who could have helped, a military trained medic stopped within seconds of the accident. It was he who recognized the signs of a broken neck, took command, and kept other good Samaritans with good intentions from ignorantly but prematurely moving Mo and possibly paralyzing her. Or worse.

The encounter occurred at 1:30 a.m., the exact time the Lord called her dad home. Clearly, God answered Mo when He heard her pray, "Wreck my life." At the same time she felt the presence of the Holy Spirit, she simultaneously sensed her *dad's* presence. It was so vivid that she could almost smell him. Touch him. Hear him say, "I've got you!" At that moment, the rebellious car immediately came to rest upside down in the ravine, yet, she felt peace flow through her like a river.

Since childhood, Mo had been a Christian, but in anger, she had not just backslidden. She had sprinted from the B-I-B-L-E: her Basic Instruction Before

Leaving Earth. When she was younger, she had merely gone through the motions, her Christianity performance based. Now she sought a personal relationship with Jesus Christ and wanted to grow in love with Him.

REHAB

Mo underwent intense rehab while rebuilding her relationship with Jesus. The result: a transformed life and a redesigned reason for living. She felt the Holy Spirit nudging her to live boldly and courageously. That required a major change. She had played it safe most of her life, trying new things only when success was certain. Now she would be strong. Be courageous (Joshua 1:9).

Praying without ceasing, God spoke back. It wasn't an audible, public address-sounding voice Mo heard, but a still, small one that's very real yet hard to explain. So she put thoughts to words in a blog, sharing her internal battles that challenged her faith and God's responses.

Gradually, Mo became comfortable sharing her back pages—the highs and lows of her story. Good or bad. Things she could not control. In brokenness, her anger and grief subsided. God had gotten her attention. She almost died. Now she died to self.

FOOTBALL

Growing up, Mo learned Christians should walk by faith and not by sight, and now the Holy Spirit was telling her to do the same. She felt convicted. She hadn't done that very well. She knew the Holy Spirit was leading her to play football again. For the first time, she didn't know how the game would turn out.

She ran the idea by her mom, who was supportive but threw a flag. If she got hit by a lineman the size of her dad, she would probably rethink the decision. Taking the idea to the next level, Mo contacted a former kicker and other football players, seeking their input about the logistics of her trying to make the team as a kicker. Once she had a discussion with the strength and conditioning coaches, they also showed their support. And then she turned to prayer. She implored, "Lord, if this is the path you have laid out for me, then let everything go smoothly. However, if I have misunderstood your signs, then halt it. Slam this door shut in front of me and make it clear that this is not the way."

She aspired to follow in her father's footsteps, to emulate the footballers who'd left him in awe week after week. He believed she could play football then, but he didn't want her to be injured for soccer season. A decade later, she was ready to come back into the game.

Mo took the goal of kicking for LSU to a higher level. She presented her idea to the assistant director of football operations, who responded with some straight talk. She couldn't play football and soccer in the same year. She could, however, finish out her soccer career, then play football in her fifth year. Then, the elephant in the room. She was a woman. And she wasn't talking about The Beatles hit song. Mo knew women's sports and women's sports history.

Mo was not the first woman to try to play college football. In 1997, Liz Heaston represented Willamette University, while Ashley Martin played for Jacksonville State University in 2001. Katie Hnida, on the other hand, kicked for both Colorado and New Mexico. However, Hnida claimed to have been a victim of sexual assault by her teammates at Colorado, although she chose not to pursue legal action. The man who held the keys to Mo's football future looked at her and said, "This isn't Colorado."

FOOTBALL PLAYER

Mo began frequenting the equipment room, requesting footballs and tees. Despite her kicks successfully passing through the goal posts, they were too low to avoid being blocked during a live game. One day, a long snapper gave her some advice—she needed to hop forward with her plant foot. This minor tweak would make her kicks rise quickly enough to clear the line. He also advised her to keep her upper body upright because, unlike in soccer, where she would lower her entire body to direct all her energy towards the ball, she needed to stay upright to gain height on a football. She grasped these changes instantly and soon started taking turns with the other kickers.

Mo excelled in both soccer and football drills. She turned up every afternoon alongside the new football recruits. Mo ended her soccer career as a goalkeeper, setting school records in wins (43), shutouts (30), saves (235), and goals against average (0.86).

When spring football practice rolled around, Mo was given a two-day tryout in March. Unfortunately, her performance was far from impressive. Her effort was admired, but there was no spot on the team. She understood. She would be back for fall tryouts. Despite the questions and smack, Mo was focused. At the practice facility, she was either on the field or in the weight room. With one difference. They were on the team. She wasn't.

With practice she got better, hitting four in a row from 35 yards. She moved back to the 40 and nailed three out of four. What jumped out among the coaches was her consistently splitting the uprights from 51 yards. She was ready for tryouts with three weeks to spare.

Finally, the day arrived. Biblically speaking "the day" sometimes refers to the day of God's judgment on the world. On this summer day, LSU's judgment would fall on Mo. Specifically—her right foot. The one that kicks field goals. Albeit at practice. But how would she do in games?

The opportunity was hardly handed to her. For eighteen months she'd worked to get to this point. Her perspective was one of acceptance. She could kick well enough to make the team, but understood there may not be enough roster spots for another placekicker. Either way, she was going to be at peace. Mo only wanted what was best for LSU. The following Friday, the SEC, Division I football team's first female to ever try out was let go. She had kicked well, said head coach Les Miles. There simply wasn't another spot for another placekicker. Her determination had drawn nationwide media attention. There had been appearances on ESPN, Fox, the *Ellen DeGeneres Show* and many other television, radio, and social media programs. Focused and passionate, she had lived boldly and courageously for Christ Jesus.

LIVING COURAGEOUSLY

Mo's cleats are permanently hung up. In Cajun, her old self "ain't no mo'." A highly sought-after motivational speaker and author, Mo shares her testimony not only across the country, but also around the world. Her candid, fascinating manner of speaking motivates audiences to overcome life's challenges and live courageously. Her feet are firmly planted on the mission field. But with one big difference. Her feet are now paired with another pair.

Married in 2014, Mary Morlan "Mo" Isom Aiken and family surrendered all, sold everything, and now minister to groups throughout the United States. Mo, a *New York Times* best-selling author, and her husband Jeremiah, with their tiny teammates Auden, Asher, Ronan, and Elijah, now kick in the kingdom of God.

We can all help prevent suicide. The 9-8-8 Lifeline provides 24/7, free and confidential support for people in distress, prevention and crisis resources for you or your loved ones, and best practices for professionals in the United States.

HELP & SUPPORT FOR BULEMICS

https://www.nationaleatingdisorders.org. Or, email, info@NationalEatingDisorders.org

RESOURCES

Gary Laney, Reporter, "Mo Isom won't play football for LSU after all." *GeauxTigerNation*, August 24, 2012.

Jason Kirk, "LSU's Mo Isom Wouldn't Be First Woman To Play College Football." *SB Nation.com*, March 6, 2012.

Jordan Ritter Conn, "Let It Fly." *Grantland*, August 21, 2012.

"LSU Roster Isom." *LSU Sports*, n.d.: lsusports.net/sports/sc/roster/player/mo-isom/M.

"Mo Isom." *Family Christian.com*, n.d..

"Mo Isom—Keynote Speaker for 2018," Annual Prayer Breakfast, *Charleston Leadership Foundation*, November 1, 2018.

Sharie King, "Mo Isom: Eating Disorders, Identity, and Calling, E7," March 2018, in *Overcoming Monday with Sharie King*, podcast, MP3 audio, https://open.spotify.com/episode/6ElhlSAGQm 4LpQUEgCjpiH.

Susan Vanselow, freelance writer and editor, "Speaking Up! Mo Isom is speaking up about sex and the need to redeem it for God's glory—realizing that our value is not defined by a partner, but by our heavenly Father." *Just Between Us Magazine*, n.d., JustBetweenUs.org.

LIFE IN JESUS

When you accept Christ, you are born again spiritually, receiving a new life in Christ. This new life is marked by a deep, personal relationship with God through Jesus. In John 3:3–7, Jesus talked about the necessity of this spiritual rebirth for entering the kingdom of God. "Jesus replied, '... Humans can reproduce only human life, but the Holy Spirit gives birth to spiritual life.'" Christ lives in you, guiding you through the Holy Spirit toward a deep relationship with Him where you can know Him intimately as your Father, Brother, and Friend.

A Christian's life is full of love for God, for oneself, and for others. In John 10:10, Jesus said, "I have come that they may have life, and have it to the full" (NIV). This suggests that Jesus's teachings are not just about securing a place in heaven, but also about leading a fulfilling, abundant life here on earth.

Living in Christ can be worry free. In Matthew 6:25–34, he taught, "That is why I tell you not to worry about everyday life—whether you have enough food and drink, or enough clothes to wear. Isn't life more than food, and your body more than clothing?"

In essence, life in Christ is about experiencing a profound spiritual transformation that impacts every aspect of your life. It's about cultivating a personal relationship with God, living life fully in Him, and experiencing the hope and assurance that comes from God's promise of eternal life.

You Can Know God Personally

To have a personal relationship with Jesus Christ, first get down on your knees. If you are not physically able to do so, humble your heart before the Lord. Then, sincerely pray out loud, the prayer below and mean it in your heart:

> Dear Lord Jesus,
> I know I am a sinner.
> I believe You died for my sins.
> Right now, I turn from my sins.
> and open the door of my heart and life.
> I confess You as my personal Lord and Savior.
> Thank You for saving me. Amen.

Did you pray this prayer?

If you said yes, you are now born again! Your old life is dead. You have been made new. You are a new creation in Christ Jesus. Congratulations! You have received the free gift of eternal life.

We want to send you a copy of the Beginner's Bible free of charge! For more information and to receive your copy, email your name and address to SinfulPrideMinistries@gmail.com.

ABOUT THE AUTHOR

Billy Zeh is a native of Northern Virginia. He attended public schools before starting a career in public service. In 1985, he and his family moved to Brunswick, Georgia, where he became a senior instructor at a training center—teaching communication skills, interviewing, stress management, PTSD, situational awareness, crisis intervention, and more.

Billy gave his life to Jesus Christ in 1988, when a Christian coworker invited him to lunch and led him to make a decision to follow Jesus. But his commitment was superficial at best, and his sinful pride graveyard deep at its worst.

Billy's transformation from being dead in sin to living a resurrected life began through a series of professional highs and lows, personal loss through a failed marriage, destruction of his family, and destruction of his home. As his good friend Keith H. observed, Billy was "the architect of his own demise." One Saturday morning the burden of his collapsed personal and professional life was too much to bear. Billy got down on his knees and asked the Lord to help him. At that moment he felt a surge of heat cover the left side of his face. A bright light illuminated the room for several seconds, then disappeared. From head to toe he felt a change encompass him. Since then, Billy has completely surrendered control of his life to the Holy Spirit, his Wonderful Counselor, the Mighty God.

Contact Billy

SinfulPrideMinistries@gmail.com

ACKNOWLEDGEMENTS

I have much to be thankful for. I can do nothing apart from Jesus. It is only by the Holy Spirit's power that this book is written. My Wonderful Counselor has guided me every day, every step of the way. I can't say "Thank You, Jesus. Thank You, Holy Spirit" enough.

Throughout my life, by God's grace and mercy, people were placed in my path to guide me in the way I needed to go, listen to me, and be a source of comfort and joy. Yes! Comfort and joy—like my brother Al did for me at Thanksgiving and Christmas. I'm not able to name them all, and some are no longer here. But I am eternally grateful to them, and to:

My late sister Mary Jo, who zipped up my snowsuit, encouraged my puns, and dragged me along on dates with her future husband, Marty Wall, who became a brother to me.

Pastor D. R. Alexandra, who is both soldier and angel.

Bill Hendrickson, who taught me to never trust a gypsy.

Craig and Susan Floyd, who treated me like a member of the family.

Richard and Julie Aldridge, who to this day include me like a family member.

Tod and Paula Donovan, who shared a spare Jekyll Island room and many great dinners.

Bruce and Suzanne Clements, for inviting us to church and entertaining my kids.

John and Kristy Bennett, Blair, and Brock, who reached out to me during the holidays.

Clint Day, my brother in Christ and his family, who sheltered me during stormy weather.

Amazing friends Earl and Lula Buckner, who are definitely blessed and highly favored

My brother in Christ Bob Kowalczyk, who has closed more books than I've read.

Harold Goddard, a prayer warrior, mighty man of God, and brother in Christ.

The unknown Chick-Fil-A entrepreneur who encouraged me to write.

Randy and Gail Ashurst, for their gift of friendship.

David and Jane Latner, for their love, witness, and Christian friendship.

Bill and Jeannie Hoffman, for their Christian love, service, and fellowship.

Cheryl Mosher and Lori (John) Durham, for editing my articles.

Sally and Gerry Hanan and their staff and Inksnatcher.com.

My God-given children Reid, Brian, and Katey, and my grandchildren, all whom I love dearly.

And Dee—Peter kept knocking. And so do I (Acts 12:16).